# SPRING TURNS

# TOO SOON

# TO WINTER

BY

JOHN WELDON EVANS

With best wishes!!.
John W Evans

Copyright © 2010 by TJMF Publishing

Printed and Bound in the United States By
Publisher's Graphics, LLC

Cover Design by Jim Furber

ISBN Number: 098-29447-8-0
13 digit ISBN Number: 978-0-9829447-8-3

Library of Congress Number: 2010935003


TJMF Publishing

TO MY SISTER

F E R M I N A

# Contents

# Winter Poems ...........................193

## Introduction

In this collection the poems are written in standard metrical style using rhyme as well as blank verse, as in the selections "The Laughing Boy," "I Am a Dreamer," "I Never Walk Alone," and "The Old Men's Club." The author writes about his observations, perceptions, and reflections on human life and on nature, often comparing them. It is hard to separate the two.

He has divided the work into eight sections, the first appropriately called "Spring Poems" and the last, "Winter Poems" for the first and last cycles of life. As in nature, all life's events take place between these two cycles, thus, the title of the book, *Spring Turns Too Soon to Winter*.

In the sections subtitled, respectively, "Spring Poems," "Summer Poems," "Autumn Poems" and "Winter Poems," the author implicitly, sometimes overtly, relates the changing phases in life to the seasons in nature, spring being equated to youth, summer to early adulthood, autumn to later adulthood and winter to old age. The author accepts the view that we are part of the pulse of nature and therefore integrated and connected somehow to its rhythms and transformations, physically as well as spiritually. For this reason he frequently addresses life and nature as if they are one. He associates the blooming of new flowers to our birth or rebirth; the exuberance and richness of spring and summer to the richness and frolic of youth and young adulthood; the seriousness and maturity of later adulthood to the mellowing of late summer and early autumn; the philosophical and contemplative withdrawal into senior years to the retreat of late autumn and early winter; and the quiet, reflective last stage of life, characterized by the acceptance of the inevitable, to late winter. These themes are directly referred to and are expressed in the poem, "Spring, Summer, Autumn, Winter."

The poems about love relationships could easily be included in the same section as "Spring Poems" or "Summer Poems," since our most impressionable emotional and romantic encounters occur in our spring and summer years (again using the seasons as analogy); nevertheless, they are placed in a separate section devoted to them, entitled "Love Poems."

Since the book is a collection, many poems written during the summer years, or young adult years of the writer's life—such as the sixties and seventies when there were heightened racial protests and social unrests in America—are grouped into a section called "On The Way to Freedom" and "Along the Way" that reflect the writer's reactions to social events and everyday life experiences during that time period. It is apparent that the sixties and seventies had a great impact on the writer's views and perceptions at that time, a fact which can be inferred from the poems themselves.

The section called "Soul Poems" deals with the author's coming to grips later in life philosophically and spiritually with the impact that separation has on relationships—a theme that obviously becomes more pronounced during the late autumn and early winter years (when most leaves are falling off the trees!). For this reason "Soul Poems" is placed between the autumn and winter sections.

As one can observe, the first poem in the collection is named "When with a Sigh or Whisper" and refers to the renewal of life that is spring, whereas the last poem is titled "Winter Sonnet" and refers to death and rebirth, tying together the recurring cycles in nature; and, as the author believes, in human existence as well.

Spring Poems

## When with a Sigh or Whisper

When with a sigh or whisper
soft and dying snow
surrenders quietly, reluctant still to go,
as if departing, even for snow,
must be the hardest thing to do;

when after twilight breaking,
a bright, sweet-tempered dawn
smiles as it sees the snow move on
after a lengthy sojourn
that buried past hopes in the ground;

when that a fresh, fluffed bud
peeks out from its drear prison,
as from a dungeon into light arisen,
and in the air a sweet sensation breeds
that multiplies and touches where it leads,

then from the spell that winter casts
earth comes alive again at last—
fields, plains and hills surrounding
and every creature living
echo in silence or with singing:

"It's spring! It's spring! It's spring!"

## Without Spring

Maybe we can't hear bluebells ring,
but we can sure hear warblers sing!
Maybe groundhogs don't know anything
but have a peculiar fling for spring!

How does a blossom know to bloom
or a butterfly to burst its cocoon?
Well, I tell you, if I know anything,
it has to do with the magic of spring.

How do swallows know the time of year?
Or hibernators when to leave their lair?
What makes a grizzly know to shed hair?
Most likely it senses spring in the air!

How tragic if they all were wrong,
if nature's clock became unwound
or stopped, and wintry snow on the ground
never left, and the whole cycle broke down!

What would we do if there were no flowering?
If there were no warblers and robins to sing?
Well, I tell you, if I know anything,
There'd be no point to living without spring.

## Let Me Drink the Rapture of Spring

Look around and listen keenly,
spring excites the atmosphere.
You can savor it freely,
it is throbbing everywhere.
Life is full, drink of it deeply,
with your senses drink your share.

From the soaring heights of heaven
to the breast of earth below,
all that lie within are laden
with spring's wondrous overflow.

When the world began the first day,
I believe was in the spring,
for, to start life's odyssey
there could be no better beginning
than to greet the heart this way
or the soul and bid it sing.

If the world started in winter,
there would be no point to spring,
and the spirit would surrender
long before it learned to sing.

Thank heaven for sunlight streaming,
for the gladness of the rain,
for the joy in all things beaming
that this season brings again!
In the streets gay sounds are peeling
this voluptuous refrain:

"Drink, drink gladly! Drink, drink madly!
Drink the rapture I bring you
till your depth is sated fully
and your heart drunk from its brew."

Beauty's in the wide sky smiling
iridescent poetry;
nature's in the parks inviting
you to share her purity.

Even mute structures surrounding
are alive with harmony.

Lofty skyscrapers o'er hanging
give an air of majesty,
of unbounded dreaming, searching
to find immortality.

Nightfall comes with its own blending
like a rapturous serenade.
Its enchantments are revealed in
quite a mystical parade:
starlight gleaming, moonlight streaming
on earth's silhouette cavalcade.

Day has magic, but the violet
touch of night mysteries unfolds;
earth by daylight wears her trinkets,
but by night she wears her soul.

All the bliss there is in living
cannot hold in one small room,
cries for space, demanding, piercing
through the walls of trivial gloom
till the heart, drunk from receiving,
swells to bear its treasures soon.

Spring, it seems, does not allow
her splendors to be shrugged away.
Night ends, dawn's new flood of joy
bursts in on our human play.

What is pain 'mid so much pleasure?
Never speak that word again.
What is love if not the treasure
of a soul's boundless domain—
all of our mortal endeavors
flow from it and back again.

Let me taste this vintage sating
every nerve and vein I own;
let me drink this wine inflating
my soul till in it I drown.

## If You Ask Me What Is Spring

Spring is nature harmonizing,
truth and beauty intertwining,
heaven and earth in chorus singing,
universal love beckoning,
promises richly o'er flowing,
glorious tidings echoing
joy to all mankind.

Spring is nature's way of giving
color to the joy of living,
new hope to the spirit grieving,
blessings to the heart believing,
sweetness to the soul forgiving,
praises to the undeceiving,
love to all mankind.

Spring is nature's way of saying
to the proud life sometimes straying,
to the contrite heart that's praying,
to the soul that's old and graying,
to the young hearts sprightly playing,
to the lovers love repaying,
"There is hope yet for mankind!"

## To a Songbird

Charmer of dryads! Melodious bird!
What sweet strains you weave high up in the trees.
What is the cause of your bliss, wondrous bird?
Can it be that the blossoms and flowers of spring,
the green earth, warm sunshine and gentle breeze
are what inspire you to sing?

Most marvelous songster in the shape of a bird,
free spirit endowed with a golden art,
what fields and forests lately heard
you thrill the dew-filled morning air?
Your strains are made to melt the heart
and blend with beauty what we hear.

Troubadour of the trees, noble bard among birds,
pouring forth from the depths of your breast with such ease
unpremeditated songs without words,
what faint heart would not leap for joy
when cascading notes fall out of the trees
in spellbinding melodies you employ?

O happy minstrel, sweet-throated bird,
melt now my heart with your musical stream.
What a loss it would be if this earthly world
knew not, blithe spirit, the bliss that you bring.
Beauty and joy might never have been
if it were that a songbird could not sing.

## The Birds of Spring

In spring you can hear all the little ones
stirring in their nests crying *tweet tweet, tweet*
as their parents return from gathering food
to fill their bellies with enough to eat.

All spring and summer they grow and grow,
keeping parents busy every day like a ferry,
back and forth with flies, beetles, grubs, worms
and everything good that their stomachs can carry.

Back and forth, miles they travel
in the fields and bushes, no time to tarry;
they must feed their young to grow strong for the journey.
Parents' lives are so tough, no rest for the weary!

By the time summer ends, the kids are grown,
their muscles are strong, their wings are well tested.
Yes, they're full grown, well trained to be on their own
while their parents are glad at last to be rested

and ready to join up with the gathering flock
of their kind getting ready to fly away south!
If you listen you can hear their chatter and shouts,
"Get into formation, find your places, we're moving out!"

Then you see the most beautiful *v*-shaped formations
as flock after flock are skyward bound,
until next spring when the travelers return
again to the woodlands, their old stomping ground!

Does this sound familiar? It certainly should!
We are no different, we humans, in many ways;
we raise our young ones and train them well
for the journey of life to the end of our days!

## Rue Paul the Fledgling Goose

One day the fledgling goose, Rue Paul,
full of curiosity and gall
asked his grandpa, the old gray goose,
questions you never should ask a goose!
"Grandpa, Grandpa, why do birds fly?
How long do birds live before they die?
And when they die, where do they go?
Where do they go, Grandpa, do you know?"

"My little gosling, you're much too young
to be asking questions so profound!"
"I know, Grandpa, but even so,
tell me the answers, I want to know!"
"First of all, munchkin, all birds must fly!
From very young they must take to the sky
the way their ancestors have always done,
to seek food where it can be found

and to stay clear of danger all around
from predators who are lurking on the ground.
As seasons change, birds must move on
to climates and pastures that are beyond
the hills and the oceans, and if they
didn't fly, there'd be no birds today!
As for how long before we die,
there are many things that birds of the sky

have to look out for. One is a hunter's gun!
If one of them doesn't shoot you down,
if you don't by mistake fly into a wall
or a building that is standing too tall,
if a speeding car doesn't hit you on the highway,
or an airplane doesn't crush you one day,
if raccoons, foxes or snakes on the prowl
or hawks and falcons who like to eat fowl

don't catch you. (Hopefully they won't!)
And if diseases don't kill you, or pesticides don't,
and hurricanes, floods, and ice storms don't get you
and you manage to survive all these things, I bet you
you might just live to be twenty-three

like an old gray geezer just like me;
and you might die in your sleep if you are lucky,
or plummet from the sky, too old to make the journey!

But don't you worry your head that you won't survive!
Even humans have problems staying alive!
They die every day, too, from guns, drugs, and wars
that destroy countless lives and inflict countless scars!
And they have epidemics, too, catastrophes and disease,
so don't think that they are immune by being humans,
please!
All species are victims to one thing or another,
but I wouldn't change my life for any other!

As for your last question, my answer is this:
If humans can go to a place of perfect bliss
when they die after all that they have done
on this earth, being that they are no paragons,
why then, they certainly must let birds like us in!
The worst we have done is fly around, honk and swim
and I never heard of a goose that ever did sin!
With no guilty conscience then, a goose got to get in!"

## Sweet Hyacinth

Sweet Hyacinth of perfume fine,
smiling with such felicity,
while cares and tears plague humankind,
you fill the air with frail beauty

and never seem to count the hour
or fuss the least about your life!
It must be blessed being a flower
unscarred by hatred, sorrow and strife!

But would you keep a smiling face
if you knew your days soon shall end?
That all your lovely charm and grace
by morrow shall have perished then?

What is your secret, gentle flower?
Whisper it to me in my ear!
"O foolish mortal, time will devour
time, yet not touch one charm I bear,

for it is not how long I live
that will determine my true measure;
I am a flower, and I give
my beauty for the world to treasure,

my nectar to attract the bees
who help to see my kind preserved!
So I have reasons to be pleased
that my purpose in life is served!

Time is a trick by fools invented
to cause their race to fret away;
so let my hour be well invested,
and you can fret away your day!"

14

**If You Should See A Lady Fair**

A lovely lady Nature has grown
gaily her crimson beauty spread,
as if for her sunlight had shone
and springtime must have raised its head.

She smiled as if to say she owned
her fate, and grief to her was unknown.
She seemed a queen upon a throne,
though soon her brief reign would be gone.

I came along and saw her then
and wondered if at all she knew
that time would soon announce her end,
and there was nothing she could do.

But she returned a smile to me
as if to say she held the key
to time and immortality
that frowns on my philosophy.

I wondered then if through this flower
Heaven had sent a message of hope,
that came not in great pomp and power
but as a sweet, harmonious note.

Surely, time measures not the worth
of this fair flower here gone tomorrow!
Brief though the space between its birth
and death, what matters anyhow?

Many may live and count their years
but have no more, when all is done,
to show for life but grief and tears,
and leave no joy before they are gone.

But this, this flower so fleeting,
more than its dues has paid today;
and will continue to make hearts sing
as long as nature has its way.

## Gardenias

Sweet gardenias, flowers that bloom
against a luscious field of green,
when plucked their fragrant petals groom
the hair of many a beauty queen.

Their creamy white, pink, yellow hues
enrich our gardens and wedding decor,
and as boutonnieres are often used
to adorn bridegrooms, best men, and more.

Gardenias, they convey such joy
to whom you give them and think much of.
If you are lost for words, feeling coy,
they can express your secret love.

I love gardenias for their sweet perfume,
their exotic nature, berries, foliage, too,
for the warmth and the magic they bring to a room,
but especially because they say, "Be true, be true."

## Not Only Flowers Are Miracles

Imagine, only yesterday
this flower, just a tiny bud,
unblown, unborn, embosomed stood!
And now it spreads its beauty gay,
unrivaled in the sun's bright rays!

It lifts its head as if to pray,
sifting the air, giving the air
a perfume for its bill of fare!
This is a miracle I say,
but all the world is just that way!

People are born to blossom, too,
like flowers in the eyes of God
from infancy's unfolding pod.
The world has known so many who
have given their beauty bright and true!

## O Bless the Hand That Painted Flowers

Bright sunny skies look down from heaven,
and everywhere beauty bursts through;
the gorgeous blooms of May have risen,
the gentle breeze caresses you.

A host of flowers on stems and vines
in gay profusion raise their heads,
basking with confidence in sunshine
amidst the greenery nature spread.

They smile as if to say they own
the garden, and this day is theirs;
they seem like queens, each on a throne
surrounded by their courtiers.

Standing awhile I watch them there,
each like a sweet harmonious note
in color from another sphere,
bringing greetings of joy and hope.

I know of no sad thoughts of ours
their beauty could not wipe away.
O bless the hand that painted flowers
in all the glory they display!

## On Hearing Two Lovebirds in the Woods in Spring

Sing! Sing your hearts out songbirds, sing!
Your gift is song, your stage is spring!
Up from the fountains in your breasts,
pour out your songs until the wind,
that famous courier of swiftness,
shall send your message echoing

to all the earth awakening
into a dream from dreaming!
O boldly let your rich pipes play
and yield charms unabating;
a cozy nest, not far away
in paradise, is waiting!

Sing, tune-swept hearts! Sing, creatures blessed
for paradise is a noble quest!
All nature and I, too, witness
your vows and your sweet trilling!
Soon you will realize the bliss
that comes from love fulfilling!

Pray, may your rich strains ever flow
till all the world with gladness glow
from such enchantment! Your duet
teaches a heart the way to sing,
and shows a soul how to forget
the scars that often to life cling!

## One Sunny Day

One sunny day as I was on my way
filled with thoughts that in hindsight seemed absurd,
I said, "There is no beauty in this world,
and truth is like a victim on display!"
I judged the world by what I read that day,
by gruesome deeds and crimes that had occurred!
Walking, I heard a voice that in me stirred
when I observed a beautiful array
of flowers that along the wayside bloomed!
O how I was so glad I passed that way—
those precious flowers bloomed so radiantly,
they greeted me like sunbeams a dark room,
and I forgot what I had read that day.
"Beauty exists," I said. "There, look and see!"

## O for the Days of Springtime

Springtime! O springtime!
Beautiful springtime,
when songbirds are singing,
butterflies are winging,
branches are grooming
and flowers are blooming,
O beautiful days of springtime!

Springtime! O springtime!
Beautiful springtime,
when new life is teeming,
and new hope is beaming,
when sunshine is glowing
and gardens are growing,
O happy days of spring!

Springtime! O springtime!
Happiest time of all time,
when carefree and spry
we were young and shy,
learning to fly
in life's purple sky,
and days bordered on the sublime!

Springtime! O springtime!
Happiest time of all time,
how quickly it went by,
as fleeting as a sigh!
We grew up too fast
for such joys to last,
O for the days of springtime!

## The Richest Man Alive

I smile when just before the dawn
I see the first glimmer of light
rising up from the horizon
to speed away the gloom of night.

I turn away from all my cares
when I pause by a little stream
to listen to a songbird's cheers
that bring glad tidings to the scene.

I even bathe in nature's showers;
chase after fleeting butterflies;
wade among a host of flowers
and revel at the wide blue skies.

I am awed to look up at the trees
towering like giants o'er a plain,
dancing and tossing in the breeze,
laughing and courting with the rain.

And when I see a crimson sky
just when the light of evening fades,
or view night's starry depths on high,
I marvel at things God's hands have made.

I own no mansions, vast domains,
no stellar stocks in the exchange,
no private yachts or private planes
and struggle with bills and with small change;

But I have family, friends, blessings
that fill my heart with joy and love;
and am thankful for all the things
that I had almost lost sight of,

for even without wealth to buy
grand things and goods men pile so high,
with just a humble heart and eye,
I think no man is richer than I.

# Love Poems

## When It Comes to Courting

There are things you see in nature
to inspire and amaze,
such as how birds choose a partner
and their fascinating ways.

For example, take a sparrow
who works hard to build a house,
then stands outside, that poor fellow,
trying his best to get a spouse!

He calls out to female sparrows,
"Come and see my pretty house!"
If one female likes it, kudos,
he has found himself a spouse.

The king bird of paradise, now he
is one impressive sight, bar none!
Tail quivering, chest fluffed up, deftly
he swings like a swinging pendulum.

I don't know what the female thinks,
but never has she seen before
such brilliant acrobatic feats
and falls for it, you can be sure,

but if you think the king is something,
you haven't seen anything until
you've seen the red-cap manikin
put on a floor show that could kill!

He flies off, returns, wings flapping
and swoops down on a branch nearby,
then does the greatest moon walking
to catch a moonstruck female's eye;

and she, curious and fascinated
comes closer and closer to see.
Then she cannot leave; she's checkmated,
and the two start a family.

Of course we know how the robin sings
and the female answers if she likes his tune.
Winged Caruso stretches his vocal strings
and before you know it has a bride in June!

Now the African lovebirds of the parrot family,
they kiss, pass food from beak to beak,
engage in foreplay and then get busy.
They are serious, too, and marry for keeps.

They are not the only ones that take
the marriage vows and bonding to heart;
the Canadian goose makes a pact with its mate,
and the trumpeter swan, "Till death do us part!"

And there are many more species, I suppose,
that bond together for a very long time.
While, on the other hand, there are those
who are just looking to have a good time.

They pair just for sex and then disappear,
like the sage grouse, sandpiper, and humming bird;
but they're not the most promiscuous, for there
are the swallow and the Australian wren—take my word.

Birds also practice polygamy
like the red-winged blackbird and the meadowlark,
and some even go in for polyandry
like the phalarope, who makes males do housework,

She runs around multiple mating!
She leaves behind for each of her mates
the jobs of incubating and housekeeping
while she goes off on secret dates.

Birds are more amazing than I can say,
and I wonder which species, bird or man,
is better at courting. Anyway,
birds are more colorful by nature's plan!

## The First Time That I Searched for Love

The first time that I searched for love
I honestly had no thought of
the treachery in a young girl's heart;
but I was slow right from the start.
She said to me, "Yes, I love you!
Sit here with me, as lovers do,
while soft winds blow beneath this tree
and I am cold as you can see!
Come, play my gallant lover's part,
draw close beside me—for a start!"
I blushed at her and blinked my eyes,
and then she whispered, "Aren't you wise?
Or maybe you don't realize.
I flushed inside, I stuttered, stared;
I wished to hide but never dared;
my manly pride wouldn't compromise;
and then she held me by the hand.
Oh, how I tried hard to withstand
the pressure of her smooth, soft hand!
I moved involuntarily
and who'd believe that, instantly,
I gasped for breath for dear, dear life;
and for awhile I helpless sat,
then flushed a smile and wondered what
would happen next to raise my strife.
Amazed, she said, "Oh, darling, why
are you so shy?" My pulse was high;
I did not move, though I did try.
She looked at me; I looked at her.
Her hands clasped me; I strained to stutter,
"D-d-darling, the m-m-moon has left the sky!"
I tried to smile and twitched my lips
and then she gave me a great, big kiss.
Oh glory be, that was the end
of bashfulness for me since then!

## The Laughing Boy

When love was a stranger to the heart,
and passion was light years away,
a boy could always smile and laugh
at the follies of grown up men.
A boy's heart was an instrument
for the wind to pluck like a roving minstrel's strings—
his mind was a mirror of unashamed simplicity.
Then did it seem that men who walked in limbo
were of another species, of another planet removed!
When scarlet sins were yet unheard of,
when swerving hips, pulsating lips,
seductive eyes were still unknown,
a boy would smile and boldly laugh
at the follies of grown-up men;
but the folly of a laughing boy
is that he, too, shall be a full grown man
and Passion's slave!
O plague of manhood, pluck these entrails now,
devour this heart and sate your appetite!
When love first came, how innocent she looked,
how charming with such coy ways
and promises of joys fulfilled!
And she was the queen of Sheba,
Cleopatra and Nefertiti all in one!
She conquered with a kiss—and soon
grew tired as her fancy changed.
O woe to him who, unaware, mistakes mere flesh
for truth and beauty like the flowers that bloom!
O woe is the heart that knows not retreat.
O pitiless is Passion that knows not defeat.
Once his palate tastes the bittersweet grapes,
once he is touched by the sorcerer-like spell,
what boy can be the same?
Gone forever that boyish pride and innocence,
that unashamed simplicity,
a laughing boy shall laugh no more
nor hearken to the minstrel's strings!

## So Much That I Could Tell You

So much I long to tell you,
I wonder if I should.
If hearts were made like minds, yes,
with all my heart I would.

So much that I could tell you,
you'd never realize—
more than would fill the oceans,
or span the breadth of skies.

But hearts and minds are different.
Where one and one make two,
a mind will trust the logic;
a heart will doubt it's true!

## Dorothy

O Dorothy, sweet Dorothy,
you look so very fine,
all chocolate brown and sugary.
Tell me that you'll be mine!

O John Daly, O John Daly,
although I must confess
you have a very sweet tongue, really
I cannot tell you yes.

O Dorothy, sweet Dorothy
with eyes of amber hue,
your lips look soft and savory;
they say I must have you.

O John Daly, O John Daly,
my mother told me one thing:
let no sweet-talking Dandy
win me without a ring.

O Dorothy, sweet Dorothy,
you put me through a lot;
I have a chariot with me,
but ring I haven't got.

O John Daly, O John Daly,
then trade your chariot in.
I wish to see only
a golden wedding ring!

O Dorothy, sweet Dorothy,
you're asking for a lot,
but first it's only fair for me
to sample what you've got.

O John Daly, O John Daly,
I'm no cook shop or market
where you can sample freely—
what you see is what you get!

So Dorothy kept her virtue
for the right man to come along,
and told John Daly what he could do
with his sweet-talking tongue!

But slick Jim Dandy knew that he
could never win them all;
"The odds," he said, "are still with me.
It takes just one to fall!"

## Ivey Divey

O Ivey Divey, round and spicy
with curves where curves were meant to be,
and with a sweet rhythm when she
walked down the street so sprightly.

I was too young to court her,
but I was old enough to sigh
and feel a sudden rush of blood
when she went walking by!

I'd wait nearby a street corner
where I knew that she would have to pass,
just to see the magic of her rhythm
and the spell that it would cast

on all her suitors and admirers
so love struck, they would make some weird
catcalls, whistling, and swearing sounds
that from far could be heard.

She ate it up like pabulum
and shook her body parts the more.
She was a prize! So many suitors
that you could not keep score!

She had her pick: rich, poor, tall, short,
old, young, handsome or just fair;
but never chose a single one,
not that she seemed to care!

The chase was all she ever loved
and she played it for all it was worth.
If you asked her why she never married,
her feelings were not hurt.

She'd say, without batting an eyelash,
"Marriage would only spoil the fun,"
and kept on teasing and flirting
just so she'd turn men on.

The years went by; here's the rest of my story:
I was older when I moved to Brooklyn,
and I learned that she had moved there, too.
One day when I went walking,

I saw what looked like a ghost from the past.
"Who's that old lady?" I asked my friend
who, like me, was from the same hometown.
Not hesitating he said to me then,

"Why that's Ivey Divey, the same one,
don't you remember her?" I was stunned.
"She lives alone and is still unwed—
all her flirting days are done."

He looked at me incredulously,
"Can you believe the trick time has played?
She was once the sexiest belle around.
Now she's just a lonely old maid."

## When Love Enthralls

When love enthralls,
chains cannot hold it
or molds mold it
into this or that shape or plan.
Laws can't control it,
or despots rule it,
perhaps no power on this earth can.

When love enthralls,
we strive, we vie for it,
sometimes even die for it
or go to great lengths in its name.
We will achieve for it,
often even grieve for it
and drink potions or go insane.

Be it curse or blessing,
though we're perplexed by it,
and often vexed by it,
without love we could not endure.
Better to reap from it
bitters and sweets from it
when love enthralls, and ask no more.

## Serenade

O come with me, O come with me, sweet angel of my dreams,
I know a place in paradise by fountains and quiet streams
where all year round is spring.

O come with me, O come my love, kismet is calling us;
our star is pointing to the east and follow it we must
while love is on the wing!

O come with me, O come with me, we've naught but fear to
lose;
all that this world can do to us, declares the ancient muse,
love is what conquers all.

O come with me today, my love, let's gather ripe fruits now.
Do not delay while there are fruits still left upon the bough,
come, hasten to love's call.

O come with me, O come away, let dalliance find its way
to hearts where ages are like sighs and many make a day
and cannot rue.

But come with me, my precious, come, no less shall I love you
than flowers love the sun or bees nectar; I will be true
as truth is true.

O come with me who am not proud, I'll love you as you are
with all your blessings, all your faults no matter what they are,
for with them you're complete.

So is a rose! Although to it even if thorns may cling,
give me the flower whole lest one change should ruin everything
and make it counterfeit.

Then come with me, O come my love. My heart's a summer sky
wherein your charms shall flourish and shall never, never die!

## If We Loved Enough For Both

If I loved enough for both of us,
just for sake of argument,
you could never do any wrong
since I'll always be content
for there'll always be a song
overflowing in my heart,
and nothing in this world could ever
tear us apart.

Using the same logic once more,
as one lover to another,
if you loved enough for both of us
we could not turn on each other.
There'd be no point! Why be jealous
when already all the trust
lies in each for both of us
two times plus.

If we loved each other thus,
it must follow as no surprise,
you'd be me, and I'd be you,
and, as a preacher once advised,
"When two love enough for both, then one
could never hurt the other; likewise,
whatever may or may not come,
they already have their prize!"

## If I Could Make a World

If I could make a world,
I'd fashion it this way:
Your beauty would be the skies,
your eyes would be the stars,
your look of love the sunshine,
your smiles the prettiest rainbows;
your lips would be ripe grapes
set to profusely burst
and make the sweetest wine.

If I could make a world,
your voice would be the sound
that wakes me up at sunrise;
your words would be prized pearls,
your laughter sweet elixir
that fills with joy my spirit
to chase away all gloom.

If I could make a world,
your being would be the earth,
your curves, your shape and form
would be the hills and valleys
where I, a happy shepherd
bound to that land of bliss,
would roam both night and day.

If I could make a world,
here is the most crucial part:
Your wisdom, thoughtfulness,
the kindness of your heart,
your spirit and your aura
would be the font of life
from which all rivers flow!

If I could make a world
as I have pictured here,
I'd never seek to roam
beyond its boundaries.
On this chaotic earth,
you'd be my Shangri-la,
my very own Shambhala!

## Love's Sweet Wine

When I first kissed you gently
and tasted love's sweet wine,
the feeling never left me
that your heart gave to mine.

The fibers in my being,
the lifeblood in my veins
awakened from a dream
and have not been the same.

We kissed, and then the darkness
became a world of light
where so much warmth and gladness
turned feelings into sight.

So much enchanting sweetness
all through the night had flown.
Alas, time could not harvest
what love's sweet wine had sown!

## When You Are Gone

When you are gone, I shall remember
the way you were dressed:
the cap that you bore,
the style of your hair,
the sweater you wore,
the beads 'round your neck,
your close fitting slacks,
your smart leather boots.

When you are gone, I shall remember
the way you said hello, and I said hi,
the way that the chemistry started to flow
with a kiss upon greeting that promised more.
I shall remember our sipping some wine
which you liked and I said I shall always provide.
I'll remember your comment about the moon,
"It must be a UFO," you said,
as it vanished for a moment out of view,
and I laughed and replied, "How could that be?
Your imagination fascinates me!"

When you are gone, I shall remember:
the touch of your cheeks against my face,
the feel of my hands caressing your skin,
the taste of your lips opening for my own,
the fire of your tongue searching to find mine,
the throbbing of our breasts, sigh after sigh,
the ecstasy thrilling through our beings
while we were locked in sweet embrace,
and, oh, the longing for time to stand still
when it seemed that our hearts were about to burst
and we wanted them to, rather than subside!

When you are gone I shall remember:
the scent of your hair, your sweet perfume,
the glow in your eyes, the flush of your cheeks,
the hating to go when we wanted to stay,
the clasping again to renew our embrace
even while we were parting, for our hearts would not go
as our lips found each other again and again,
and the words kept repeating from your lips and mine,

"I love you, I love you so!"
When you are gone and the years have flown,
once in awhile when I am alone
in the quiet of a summer night,
or an autumn night before twilight,
or deep into a wintry night,
like a sweet refrain
coming back again,
these precious moments
I shall remember.

## In the Vast Ocean Eternity

How small one life appears to be
in the vast ocean eternity,
where ageless time has no end to it,
where one life is a fleeting minute
and lives uncounted are in it
like little drops that make a sea,
one drop a seeming triviality!

How like a speck one sparrow fallen from a tree
in the vast ocean eternity!
Mark how a little robin by your window pane
is singing its heart out again and again
with you drinking the sweet refrain!
Poor little sparrow time will forget,
and the robin and you shall vanish yet!

How miniscule one teardrop then must be
in the vast ocean eternity!
How fleeting one ecstatic thrill that lifts
the heart such as a lover's kiss!
How sad the pain of parting is,
yet swift, O swift that pain must be
in the vast ocean eternity!

## Remember

When glasses with rich wine are filled,
when eager hearts throb to be thrilled,
and when the band plays sweet and low
in halls where dimmed lights softly glow,
remember!

When autumn leaves turn crisp and brown
and in the winds fall to the ground,
when soft white snow beneath your feet
sinks as you walk along the street,
remember!

When truth is balanced on the scale
and time has healed where all things fail,
when everything is said and done,
and when a love at last is gone
forever,

Remember well, remember long
a "once-when-love-was-furtive" song
that moved two hearts to passions deep
and promises they could not keep!
Remember!

## Sing a Song For Me, Calluha
(To be sung while a guitar is strumming)

Strum a tune for me, Calluha,
upon your guitar, strum;
strum a tune for me, Calluha,
before the heartaches come!

Sing a song for me, Calluha,
to take away the pain;
sing a song for me, Calluha,
and let me smile again!

Tell a lie to me, Calluha,
and maybe I'll forget;
say that she and I, Calluha,
had never even met!

All the day seems gray, Calluha,
all the songs sound sad;
make them go away, Calluha,
make a sad song glad!

Strum a tune for me, Calluha,
it's the only way
to bring peace for me, Calluha,
let the music play!

Take this load away, Calluha,
beating on my brain;
on a summer day, Calluha,
better sun than rain.

Make the sky turn blue, Calluha,
chase the clouds away;
I am counting on you, Calluha,
let your guitar play.

Play, play, play, play,
send the tears away, way, way;
play, play, play, play,
what a bitter day, day, day.

42

## The Coin

He keeps it safe within his wallet
inside a secret compartment
and never takes it out, except
sometimes when he is tired and spent,

and he's alone, no one watching!
He reaches into his back pocket,
dreading this time it might be missing!
Did he replace it? Could he have dropped it

the last time he had looked at it?
He was frantic; but fortunately
his fears were quelled when he found it
and clutched it, oh, so tenderly!

If only that coin could tell the story
how from all the coins throughout the land
it was the one by destiny
that ended up in Celia's hand!

In her hands one touch and that nickel
was nevermore the same!
She gave it to him when they were little
to hold, to keep it in their name!

It was a coin that meant a dream,
a hope of two hearts long ago.
It was a coin two hearts had deemed
was their down payment for tomorrow.

"When we have saved enough," she said,
"we'll buy a castle for love to grow!"
It sounded real, so real, granted;
but what do little children know?

Not long after, her family
had packed, and they all left the town,
Then months and years weighed heavily
even on one who was so young.

He tried his best to forget her
and the dream that one day they would join;
yet it was strange he couldn't surrender
or spend that precious five-cent coin!

Grown up, he looked for her, not knowing
that she had gone to a foreign land;
and she, in turn, tried writing him
which was an all-but-hopeless plan.

One day he reached that foreign land!
It must have been the coin of fate
that worked its magic and played a hand
to lead him there; but O too late!

He mentioned her name to a friend
who knew her and who told him of
the story of Celia's sad end—
how she had sought to find lost love

in a strange land with a stranger.
It wasn't the love of long ago,
but she would make it work for her.
Alas, that brought disaster, though!

How could she know death was the stranger
far off in that distant land?
Her heart was once pledged to another
but fate dealt her a different hand.

"If you would find your Celia now,
she is lying in the cemetery.
She's gone!" Life never is, somehow,
the way children wish it could be.

He held the coin, fought back the tears,
then placed it in his wallet and
was glad he kept it all these years—
the coin that once touched Celia's hand!

**So the Beauty of Her Face**

Like a rosebud plucked too soon
before it formed into a rose;
like a book just when it opened
and fate stepped in and had it closed;

Like a promise of delight
that never saw the light of day;
like a hope that burned so bright
ere the light was taken away—

so the beauty of her face
and heart that I remember.
They will never be erased,
entombed in my mind forever.

**If Love Is True and I Am Untrue to Love**

If love is true
and I am untrue to love,
I'll never sing again!

If love is true
and I am untrue to love,
though fancies strut and tease
I'll never smile again!

If love is true
and I am untrue to love,
though dawns in splendor break
I'll never yearn to see
another morning sun rise!

If love is true
and I am untrue to love,
though fortune favors me
in every way but one—
I am untrue—
I shall be cursed!

If love is true
and I am untrue to love,
I'll never dream again,
nor stroll beneath the stars again
my hand in hand with bliss,
nor know again the softness of a summer breeze,
nor hear birds sing!

If love is true
and I am untrue to love,
I'll never lavish on another rose,
nor marvel at another sunset in the sky,
nor hear another song to charm my soul,
nor see another rainbow that can please my eye,
nor feel another burst of joy when spring returns—
for I shall never love again!

## I Never Thought That I Would Sing Again

I never thought that I would sing again
the way a happy schoolboy used to sing,
or feel in autumn that it still is spring.
The ways of love I shall not comprehend
if I should live to be a hundred ten!
Why should it seem in autumn that it's spring?
What is this sweet yet agonizing thing
that keeps a heart yearning without end?

I cannot say I never loved before,
nor played the fool, but that was long ago
and might have been a schoolboy's crush or two.
But I am wiser now and know much more—
then tell me why, for all that I know,
autumn turned into spring when I met you?

## Smitten by a Rose

I once was smitten by a rose
when visiting in a certain land.
I do not know how the heart knows
what the mind cannot understand—
how in a fleeting moment one spark
could fly across a crowded room
from that sweet rose to ignite my heart.
In God's garden of flowers that bloom,
none had I seen with such sweet grace
as if an angel's from heaven came down
and settled on a human face.

In God's garden of flowers that bloom,
none had more grace to melt my heart.
She moved so blithely across the room,
then like an arrow that found its mark,
she said to me softly, "Hurry back soon!
I hope you make this land your home."
Then I felt saddened to have to depart
and planted a kiss upon her cheek.
She seemed a child in matters of the heart
(So fresh and innocent with eyes that speak!)
I hadn't the courage or will to say

what she and I had already known
even while her eyes melted my heart away:
that when I from that land had flown
I would not see her face again
for she was to another wed;
and our flight of fancy had to end
with a tender, sad goodbye instead.
O poor dark eyes you can't help but live
like a rose so bright that men admire,
knowing your heart is not free to give
no matter how much we may desire.

## Requited Love

I stand now at the summit of my life
and contemplate where I have been and why,
and where I'm going or whether time can lie.
I count all of the scars placed here by strife,
the many travails of which this world is rife,
the moments lost, the years that have gone by,
the empty victories that oft belie
one's worth and make one march to fickle fifes!

Nothing I've seen but proves to me the more,
that vanity is not worth living for;
I've come to know a simple truth, my dear—
perhaps that wisdom is what brought me here—
life's troubles fade away in the light of
the joy and beauty of requited love!

## The Rose Garden

There is a garden of roses
sweeter than bloom in May;
ever the warmth it exposes
transcends the fetters of clay.

Fashioned, this garden of roses,
with consummate care and art,
throughout the years it discloses
beauty that comes from the heart!

When you need flowers around you
to brighten the place where you stay,
come to that garden I've grown you
and pick out a lovely bouquet!

There are roses of understanding,
roses of passion true,
roses of kindness attending
all to the love of you;

roses of friendship enduring,
roses of hope ever new,
roses of trust never failing,
all for the love of you.

Flowers that bloom in the springtime
wither and soon must decay;
but those that grow in love's sunshine
will never fade away!

## Love Is Like A Flower

Graceful is a flower
growing on a vine,
made from sun and shower
and a seed combined.
Fair and frail and fragrant,
fresh and rich and rare;
king and lowly vagrant
have found treasures there!

Love is like a flower
growing on life's vine,
made from tears and laughter
and a pledge combined.
It grows ever sacred
when it shall endure;
they have been rewarded
who have found love's shore.

## I Had Thought to Love Was Best

I had thought to love was best
if even that the burning quest
itself might not be realized!
Faced with these choices: not to love
or love purely and not be moved
by earthly powers, not even death,
I choose to love.

I had thought to love was best
and not to speak a word of love
if that might mean the only gain
is that it would save you from pain.
If my love would not be known
except by you, me, and God alone,
I still choose love.

I had thought that it was best
to love yet not to speak of love
if by so doing would keep it safe,
the world not knowing. The silence of
my secret then would hurt just me!
If that's the price that I must pay,
I choose to love.

I had thought to love was best
if there was any way that we
could capture that first perfect smile,
that first glimpse of paradise,
that first look of utter bliss
and sustain it. Once it's gone,
it's gone forever.

I had thought to love was best
if the quality of love was kept
in a pure inviolate state.
The only guarantee we'd have
that love would stay the same today
and always would be to freeze love
in time once found!

Then the greatest bliss would be
that time had frozen when we met
and that fleeting moment set.
You'd be beautiful forever,
and I'd forever worship you.
O for that glorious moment then,
I choose to love!

## A Wedding Song

(To be spoken during a wedding ceremony)

Bridegroom:
"Take my hand and let us walk together.
Let your strengths and my strengths,
your talents and my talents be as one;
and where you go, my heart shall go,
that where you are, I am also!"

Bride:
"Take my hand and let us walk together,
opening doors together, you and I;
and your joys shall be my joys,
your sorrows my sorrows,
your pain my pain!"

Bridegroom:
"Take my hand and let us walk together,
and your world shall be my world,
your people, my people;
and where you lay your head,
there I shall lay my head!"

Bride:
"Take my hand and let us walk together
over rough places and smooth places,
four footsteps in the sands of time;
and your dreams shall be my dreams,
your wishes my wishes!"

Bride and Bridegroom together:
"Here is my hand, now we shall walk together
and laugh together, and cry together!
Your treasure will be my joy, your joy my treasure
and our wealth will be each other,
and forever be as one!"

## Kumarie and Shakeem

O Shakeem, Shakeem,
true lover of mine,
sweet is the love you give;
but will you love me still
when I am old and gray?

O Kumarie, O Kumarie,
whom I dearly adore,
when you turn old and gray
as I shall, too, one day,
I shall but love thee more.

O Shakeem, Shakeem,
true lover of mine,
sweet is the love you give;
but if I'm weak and bent
and barely see, what then?

O Kumarie, O Kumarie,
my dearest, dearest love,
when that the heart shall see
't will see the same as now,
though many years are spent
and we are old and bowed.

O Shakeem, Shakeem,
my lover true,
though you do love me now,
all things, I fear, must end!
And when I'm dead and gone,
how will you love me then?

O dearest, dearest Kumarie,
my love shall never die!
If even we have changed—
as all things shall with time—
yet time will not the cheater be
for you and me,
however swift it flies!

O Shakeem, Shakeem,

sweet lover of mine,
how shall I know thee then
if we are not the same?
If we are changed, tell me,
the way that love shall be?

O Kumarie, O Kumarie,
O dearest, dearest one,
a thousand years from now
if you're an angel,
I'll be the sunshine
that warms your face divine!

O Shakeem, Shakeem,
true lover of mine,
your words and pledges sweet
are worth my sleep with thee
as long as you love me,
no matter what shall be!

My dearest, dearest Kumarie,
ten thousand years from now,
if you're a bird, I'll be the wind
that bears you up
in flight and soothes your wings.
If you're a rose,
I'll worship at your vine
and be charmed every hour
ten thousand years and more!

O Shakeem, Shakeem,
true lover of mine,
I cannot wait to see
or share such bliss with thee!
Tell me again, my love,
that it may dwell in me
tomorrow and forever!

Kumarie, my love, Kumarie,
O dearest, dearest one,
if I'm a sunflower, you'll be my sun;
if I'm a bee, you'll be my nectar;
if I'm a song bird, you'll be my song;

if I'm an oyster, you'll be my pearl!
You'll be my rainbow in my world,
my treasure and my happiness
as you are now, and I'll be blessed
ten times ten thousand years!
And though eons go by,
when you shall say to me,
do you still love me now?
Just like a star,
the brightest in the skies,
you'll sparkle in my eyes
and I'll be answering still,
"Yes, yes, my love, and always will
for all eternity!"

## Lost Love

There was once a vision of love and delight
when tomorrow was a long ways out of sight!
There was once a dream and a promise so bright
when choices and promises clashed with all their might
and the gift of a rose perished on the ground.

There was once a dream of a kingdom of our own
that might have been when the future was unknown;
but before we could grasp it, the dream was gone!
There was once a queen who was never crowned
and a king who never even sat on his throne.

There was once a fountain that time has closed;
a kingdom that sank before it arose;
a dawn that came not, though hearts were disposed;
a song that was hushed before being composed;
and a love that was lost and was never found.

### Speak No More to Me of Love

Now speak no more to me of love,
that ever veiled, illusive phantom
that I have sought, that has sought me
in every place, in every town
till it grows late and I grow weary
as now the years keep dwindling down.
Maybe it was not meant to be
for we have kept missing each other
while moving at a different pace;
but it would be another matter
if we could have met face to face
one quiet evening before the winter,
and ended this very tiresome chase!
Once, I recall, we came so close,
close as a heartbeat yet failed to capture
what nearly was, heaven only knows,
when some untimely misadventure
unwittingly had interposed.
The rule of averages, I fear,
gives but one chance for perfect bliss;
and I had seen mine disappear
into the whirlwind and the mist!

Summer Poems

## Those Barnstorming Days of Summer

There we were, in those hot summer days,
barnstorming from city to city or bust,
Boston, D.C., Montreal and Philly,
playing any and all who dared challenge us.

I was on first board, Alvin on second,
Matthew on third, Holder on fourth,
Billy on fifth board and if need for a sixth,
Jerry our intrepid captain stepped forth.

Jerry, our self appointed leader
would cause many a tempest in a teapot
by his radical, revolutionary ways in the sixties
till he scared me to death that he'd cause a riot,

challenging every cop, every racial slight
like he wanted single-handedly to start a war!
We had to calm him, tell him this was not his fight,
to save it for chess, that's what we came for,

not to start a riot, not to start a war!
He would cool his temper for a little while,
at least till the next chess match was over,
and if we won, then you'd see a smile!

Those were the good old days, I remember;
chess was our outlet that kept us up late,
playing in the streets and the parks in Brooklyn
while civil rights and revolution just had to wait!

I think we kept Jerry out of trouble, anyhow,
or he'd be leading every civil rights parade,
and we might have followed him, too, somehow;
but thank heaven we loved chess—and how we played!

Those summers are gone now, like most of the gang—
no more Alvin and Matthew and Holder and Billy!
They didn't last till winter, but the memories remain—
barnstorming in Boston, D.C., Montreal and Philly.

**Summertime**

Summertime is the time when you can see
how many people inhabit a city
and can fit on a small piece of real estate
when the lure of the outdoors brings them out!
It's a time for liberation from stuffy clothes,
for casting off all that the law allows,
though some people always go to extremes
and liberate too much in fashion's name.

Summertime is a time for butterflies and bees,
for flying balloons, paper kites and planes,
a time for Frisbees, playing catch, climbing trees,
a time for frolicking in the grass,
for strolling casually through the parks,
for skating, bicycling, motor biking,
for gay picnics, fiestas and barbecues,
for taking long drives in the countryside.

Summertime is a time for chess in the parks,
for speed chess and round robin Swiss tournaments,
for young and old men playing checkers or cards
or just sitting there relaxing in the shade
with a soothing, summer breeze blowing by!
It's a time for strollers and baby carriages
and mothers calling out while watching their tots,
while pets and young children are running wild!

Summertime is a time for trekking in the woods,
a time for hiking, building tents, campfires,
a time for sleeping under the stars
watching the myriad blinking lights.
It's a time for hunting, bird watching, exploring,
being with nature away from the city,
a time for observing creatures in the wild,
for collecting objects, pictures, memories.

Summertime is a time for water hosing,
dancing jubilantly in the pouring rain,
or being drenched by gushing fire hydrants.
It's a time for backyards and swimming pools,
a time for beaches, boat riding, sail boating,

a time for fishing on the piers
or on fishing boats beyond the point
early in the morning tasting salt sea breeze.

Summertime is a time for summer sports,
for playing volleyball, baseball, basketball
in the streets or on playgrounds, entertaining crowds.
It's a time for street vendors like the Good Humor man
selling flavored ices, sodas, ice cream cones;
or other street vendors peddling their wares
such as hats, wallets, trinkets, ladies' handbags;
or food vendors selling hot dogs and hamburgers.

Summertime is a time for air conditioning units,
for electric fans and dehumidifiers,
a time for sitting in air conditioned theaters,
in air conditioned cars, buses, subway trains
while trying to beat the heat—often suffocating.
And with all the households seeking relief,
sometimes in the summertime systems break down
and we have power shortages and blackouts.

Summertime is a time for courting, too,
for girl watching and boy watching that is no surprise.
They display their talents, their assets and traits,
like a sage grouse courts a female or a cockatoo struts,
or a peacock spreads his plumes for the female to see
all his attributes fine for the mating dance.
In nature all creatures are the same
when it comes to strutting and showing their wares.

Give me a place where I can see
the summer parade and the interchange
between people and nature and the bright displays
both are capable of, with variety
and energy, and cheers, while the earth revolves
in its preordained orbit, and the sun and the stars
light the heavens that existed so long ago,
I cannot even begin to surmise.

## Popcorns

Coming out of theatre number one
I could see, entering the main lobby,
the concession lines were very long!
It seems everyone had the same plan
to load up with snacks the best way they can
before the feature film began.
I saw a fat man struggle mightily
with two bucketfuls in one hand and
a gallon of soda in the other hand.
"Gosh, what an appetite," I thought,
"he must have a very large family!"
As I got near the front, the clerk called out
to the next person standing in line,
"Medium, large size or bucket size?
Miss, please do not hold up the line!"
"Large," said a girl with frisky eyes,
"and put plenty butter on it, beside!"
"Anything to drink?" asked the young male clerk.
"Yes, two giant Cokes!" the young girl replied.
And then it was my turn, oh, that smell!
That couldn't be popcorn; that's B.O.! I thought,
It came from the person behind me, no doubt.
"Give me two large sizes," I blurted out,
"with butter on one, the other without,
and two medium Cokes with lots of ice!"
"That will be sixteen dollars, sir!"
Good thing I had enough to suffice—
I am glad I took the special discount
when I bought the tickets coming in!
With two hands now full and enough to eat:
two 'large' sizes and two cokes, hurrying
I rushed back inside to find our seats,
and I got there just in the nick of time!
"Thank goodness," she said, my honey said,
"Here, let me give you a helping hand!
 I can't wait to get my teeth into
those succulent, mouth watering popcorns,"
as the feature film began.

## Let's Go Walking in the Park

Let's go walking in the park
just you and I sweetheart,
while flowers are blooming,
trees are grooming,
birds are singing,
squirrels are prancing,
children are dancing
and nature is orchestrating.

Let's go walking in the park
just you and I sweetheart;
and if we grow weary
we'll sit by a tree
while breezes blow gently
and we share the bliss
that we might have missed
had we stayed in the hectic city!

Let's go walking in the park
just you and I sweetheart!
We'll stop by the lake
before it gets late
and see ducks navigate
to the tranquil flowing
of the lake while we go rowing,
two lovers, me and my Kate!

## On a Peaceful Night in Summer in the Woods

Moonlight shimmering on a pond
in the night winds in the woods—
stealthy creatures make no sound
stalking unsuspecting prey!

Crickets' chirping, bull frogs' croaking
are the only sounds you hear,
then the spell is suddenly broken
when a quick retreat is foiled

and as quick the deed is done
with a pounce, a rustle, squeal!
Moonlight shimmering on a pond
in the night winds in the woods!

Crickets chirping all night long,
bull frogs croaking in a pond!
They must know life must go on
as they chirp and croak their song.

## Painted Lady

One bright and sunny afternoon, the air
was filled with fragrances of perfume everywhere!
The streets were paved in sun-drenched sheets, and on
the joy-swept sidewalks, light steps came along:
a painted lady from whom radiance shone,
with jewels in her hair that sparkled in the sun,
was walking in that summer air, stately and sure,
was walking, greeting all with smiles and with allure!
The earth appeared to rise to meet her shifting feet;
her swerving hips and shoulders moved in rhythmic beat
and yielded to the pleasing whole
their share of splendor to behold!
Upon the lawn the grass blades bowed their heads and
sighed,
"She walks! She walks in painted beauty magnified!"
I gave my heart away that summer day;
but when the paint and glitter wore away,
I longed for simple virtue, modest clay,
and not a painted lady on display!

## One Summer Night

One summer night when stars were shining bright,
when high above in silent watch, the moon
glowed from her perch, love played a furtive tune!
Upon a bank where sea breezes unite
and rippling waves are heard in soft delight
while o'er dark waters shimmering gleams lie strewn,
two lovers trysted (though their love was doomed!)
and pledged their all beneath the pale moonlight!

Hardly their stolen bliss was in their grasp
when, bittersweet, it weighed upon their hearts
sealing its own doom just when it took flight!
The lovers parted, passions cooled at last,
reason and conscience played the final part
and ended fancy's flight one summer night.

## Summer Sunshine, Summer Rain

Summer sunshine, summer rain
descending on a distant plain.
Summer smiles and summer tears,
memories lasting through the years.
O how very close we came
and never came close again!

Summer fields and gardens green,
raindrops cooling petals seen
in a rapturous summer scene!
It was there where we once met
in a place and time now set—
it is so hard to forget!

Summer wind and summer rain
beating on a window pane,
pouring out an old refrain:
"Two hearts joined together here
for a little while and then
never passed this way again!"

Summer joys and summer pain,
through the mist and through the rain.
Since then many summers came,
and seasons rolled around again;
but we'll never see the same
summer sunshine, summer rain!

## Summer Days Are Over

It's over, it's over, it's over,
days of summer are all gone!
It is now late in October,
and the love affair is done!

No more barbecues and picnics;
no more frolicking until dark;
no more street fiestas and ferias;
no more concerts in the park.

Time to put on clothes and cover
all the parts that were laid bare
in the golden days of summer,
for a chill is in the air!

No more wood pushing on park benches
till the daylight is dispersed;
no more summer barnstorming,
time cannot be reversed.

No more hiking, no more camping
under a starry sky;
no more exploring, woodland trekking,
glorious summer days, goodbye!

It's over, it's over, it's over,
all the crowds have disappeared;
time to say goodbye to nature
and to friends of yesteryear!

Very soon leaves will be falling,
and the trees will all be bare;
then the summer joys and laughter
will be memories to share!

## Boys and Girls of Summer

There was a time for boys and girls of summer
way in the long ago and far away—
a time and place that I can still remember
filled with such unrestrained joy and with laughter!

We ran about the grounds and fields all summer,
played ball between the houses all day long,
and when it rained we sailed boats in the gutter,
played marbles and "shooflao" under the cellar!

Our great skaters went racing up and down,
jumping o'er people lying on the ground;
and teenagers on bicycles had fun
while slower kids on scooters scooted along.

If they chose not to rough it with the boys,
girls played hopscotch on sidewalks or skipped rope;
and little children ran amuck with toys
while some grownups complained about the noise.

Sometimes we flew kites on a windy day
to see whose paper kite could fly the highest!
Of course often the wind had the last say
when it fiercely swept lots of kites away!

We were the boys and girls of summer then
without a serious care, or fret or fuss;
but summer's gone now, winter's round the bend
proclaiming, "Frost is on its way, my friend!"

**Until the Last Summer's End**

The end of the season was drawing near,
and flowers were fading on fragile boughs
when I saw a rose that seemed not to care
that the season was drawing too soon to its close.

It was like a miracle, as if Nature placed
all her talents in this gentle flower
and endowed her with so much beauty and grace,
the quintessence of Nature's poetic power.

Never mind that the season would soon desert her,
in the days that remained she was a queen.
Like the finest work of a master painter,
she was the brightest flower I had ever seen!

She was clothed with the tincture of a heart
and a fragrance that was from Heaven sent.
Despite her brief hour she determined to impart
to the world all her talents ere her life was spent!

I was moved and I thought, till the last summer's end
if only the human heart could remain
true to God's purpose as this rose had been,
then life's season, though brief, could not be in vain!

# On the Road to Freedom

## Poems

## How Can a Land So Full of Promise
(1963)

How can a land so full of promise
be a land filled with despair?
How can a land built on the premise,
"All men are equal," be unfair?

How can a land espouse democracy
and be a haven of hypocrisy?
How can a land by God created
be a land with so much hatred?

How can a land that preaches justice,
brotherhood, love, Christianity,
preach such things and yet not practice
what it preaches to humanity?

How can a land that welcomes gladly
all men seeking to be free
place chains on some men unjustly,
denying them their liberty?

How can a land of fertile fields
harvest fruits from bitter seeds?
How can a land of high ideals
harvest good from bitter deeds?

The sins of men are great and small
and must be answered for, one and all!
If no man can escape His rod,
how will a nation answer God?

**Who Am, What Am I?**
(1964)

I am the child, I am the flesh,
I am the flesh born of the seed
that came from the seed of a bartered slave,
who was the child born of the flesh
that came from the seed of an African
who roamed the valleys, who roamed the hills,
who roamed the valleys and the hills
of Africa long, long ago!

I am the songs, I am the songs,
I am the cries, the cries that swell,
I am the sweat, I am the blood,
I am the blood that flows, that flows,
the heart, the genius used, abused
for centuries!  Yes—countless blows
have scarred my body, mind, and soul!
I am the spirit of Africa raped and sold!

## The Angry Warrior
(1966)

He took the cup of knowledge, drank deeply,
and was instilled with truth and wisdom,
then he emerged from the dungeons of darkness
with a new calling, a quest for freedom!

Armed then with wisdom and truth on his side,
never again would he be a slave;
he was prepared to do battle, a warrior
destined to fight or to sleep in his grave!

Glowing in the light like a fiery prophet,
he was a tall, brilliant, brave warrior
piercing the air with his voice like the thunder,
echoing a pledge never to surrender

to the forces of hypocrisy,
to the authors of his people's pain,
to the robbers, brain washers, oppressors,
to the slavers who forged his chains!

And as he spoke on so many occasions,
every man, young and old, stood up tall;
his was the voice of their manhood, a nation;
his was the spirit of one and all.

When he spoke they knew a prayer was answered:
he was an instrument playing the right chord.
How youth responded and anxiously gathered
soon like an army poised to go forward.

He led the way, and the young blood, they followed.
How he struck terror in the hearts of oppressors!
He shook the very foundations they hallowed,
exposed their myths while inspiring his followers.

And, as the smoke grew thick in battle,
his enemies plotted to silence his voice;
but when a warrior goes into battle,
he faces danger without any choice!

So he went forward as only he could—
nothing could deter the mission he bore,
for he belonged to the people, the struggle,
and he resigned to what lay in store.

If you have seen a braver man, tell me!
Nothing could deter his course anymore;
so it was when in the shadows Death stalked him,
he still came forth in his shining armor!

Never was he more in his power,
never a warrior glittered more brightly,
as he confronted his final hour.
Even against Death he stood tall and mighty!

If the oppressors, the killers of men,
thought with their bullets to silence this man,
thought they could silence the hopes of a people,
when will they learn that they never can!

O vain oppressors and killers of men,
something you never could understand:
though you may kill again and again,
the spirit of Malcolm lives in every man!

## In His Image
(1967)

Born with an immortal soul,
with a heart warmer than gold,
with a mind fresh and untainted,
with a skin the Maker painted,
with two hands to clasp and hold
and a character to mold;

born with gifts too often doomed
with no chance for them to bloom,
coping with hatred and scorn
from the day when you were born,
fighting against hurts inside
with an ever burning pride;

born, God knows, to be as free
as a sparrow in a tree,
free to stretch and try your wings,
not to live with broken things
like a sparrow in a cage
with your soul burning with rage;

born to love, not born to hate,
though the world would change that fate;
born with hope and born with trust
often trampled in the dust;
born a darker child—'tis true,
in his image, God made you!

**On Reading About the Lynching of a Black Man**
(1968)

I was reading an old news story
that was very grim and gory;
it told how they lynched a black man,
imagine if you can!

They gagged and bound him tight
in the middle of the night,
crackers, honkies, redneck trash
flailing hatred with the lash!

Jigger, such a coward's night,
Klansmen dressed in hoods of white!
Murder, murder in their sight,
could not even stand the light!

They tortured, showed him no mercy!
Hanged him high up on a tree!
Then I thought of Calvary—
and Christ who died upon a tree!

**Reflections on a Painting on a Wall**
(1969)

Teardrops bright and clear,
crystals of despair,
sparkling in the dim light's glare
from the corners of dark eyes,
like they're questions in disguise,

flowing and yet lingering there
like a stain of some disgrace
that the darkness can't erase,
like a soul's bitter lament
for a promise cruelly rent!

Teardrops bright and clear
fill the silence now unbroken
like a phrase that's never spoken,
like a tragedy reflected
in an image introjected!

Teardrops in the dim light's glare
cry out to this cold, harsh place
where hate shrouds the human race,
where injustice rears its head
each day and is richly fed!

Teardrops bright and clear,
like a sadness that is seen
for the dreams that might have been,
for the hopes dashed to despair
in a world that doesn't care!

Teardrops bright and clear,
blemishes that sorrow paints
in the shadows of restraints
that can never wash away
though the canvas may decay,

for the tears that are seen there
flow within the eternal breast
where they'll never be suppressed,
where God's justice does not sleep
and rivers run dark and deep!

## Thursday, April 4, 1968
(1970)

Where was America on that fateful day in 1968,
on the afternoon of April 4 of 1968,
when a shot rang out in daylight down in Memphis,
Tennessee?
Where were the people of America at that moment that
lives in infamy?
Were they working on the late shift?
Were they traveling home from work?
Were they listening to some music on the radio?
Were they sitting in a bar or in a crowded restaurant?
Were they sitting in a theatre or in a local barbershop?
Were they walking down a busy street or riding in a bus?
Were they riding in a crowded subway train?
Were they standing on a corner on some busy city street?
Were they shopping in a grocery store or some department
store?
Were they home with family sitting 'round the dinner table
Or looking at their favorite TV show with sandwiches and
beer?

Where was America at that moment when a killer cowardly
stalked,
when a fiend, a mindless monster, reprobate,
a scaly scum, a villain, vile degenerate
crouched on a window sill with evil gleaming eyes,
with filthy fingers on a fated trigger?
Where was America that Thursday when the dreadful
trigger snapped,
when the head of him who fell in mortal agony
lay pierced upon a Memphis balcony?

And when they heard the news that evening
how did they feel inside? Were they stunned? paralyzed?
Was there a shudder, shiver deep within?

Did their hearts suddenly race and skip a thousand beats?
Did something in them die?
And did they feel as if a light had gone out of the world?
Did they cry out and hold their heads in anguish?

84

Did they shed tears and all night wonder why?
Did they feel rage that almost turned to violence?
Did they speak out and curse the seeds of racism
spread wide in this great land, nurtured by hate,
and did they curse its bitter harvest, too?

O villainy!
O blind hate and mindless villainy!
O unholy Thursday!
O April 4 of l968! O day that lives in infamy!
O America! O America!

## Ode To A Freedom Fighter
(1970)

**1**

The phantom world has gained a noble prize!
High in its martyred ranks has been inscribed
the name of one who now with patriarchs lies!
How strongly might his followers have proscribed
Death claiming him if only they could choose!
But who are we to stay the reaper's hand?
Mere mortals, proud at best, but mortals still.
Though we might wish, we cannot Death abuse
nor stay its hand. Only the Maker can—
for all things work according to His will.

**2**

Death looked at him one day and envious said,
"Live briefly now, brave heart, but come tomorrow
a bitter path awaits where you must tread,
and where you'll go, no mortal flesh can follow!"
"Why?" Earth lamented when in silent pause
it mourned the light taken that meant so much,
a light that shone so brightly in our lives!
Earth grieved its loss, perplexed by Heaven's cause.
Too cruel seemed Death's sudden, awful touch
that somehow we forgot the dream survives!

**3**

He's dead? No, no, banish baneful despair!
His spirit walks among the living still.
Wherever oppressed are gathered, he is there!
See how he rises to his feet to quell
a restless multitude that's standing by
awaiting! Now—be still! Hush! Hear him speak!
"Let freedom ring," he cries, "let freedom ring!
The dream! The dream! You must not let it die!
From every valley, every mountain peak
on earth, let freedom ring, let freedom ring!"

**The Slave**
1971

Snatched from the womb of a great continent,
wrenched from its rich umbilical cord,
torn from a land and a birthplace once cherished,
chained in despair, rage, bewilderment
deep in some vermin-infested hold,
whipped like a beast till the flesh was disfigured,
you were like cargo to be bought and sold,
shipped in scourged galleys of stinking flesh!

Though there were many daring escapes
from the dread galley holds, chains notwithstanding,
though there were warriors against untold odds
who broke for freedom and thwarted their fates,
many were butchered who were so bold!
Many were taken, commodities for trading
and were transported to markets and sold,
then carted off like mere things before God!

Branded and shackled and showered with scorn,
driven like a beast all across this great land,
prodded like a mule to work in the field
loading, unloading, picking cotton and corn,
used as a footstool, an outlet for passions,
charged not to act or to speak like a man,
slaughtered in public on festive occasions
for stepping out of your place in the field,

working from sunup to sundown each day,
watching your offspring marched off to be sold,
seeing your family abused without pity,
having no voice and no rights anyway,
having to walk in the shadow of men
who called themselves masters, and who strode
like some divine right was given to them
to practice inhumanity,

you were transplanted in this strange new land,
forced into bondage and forced to act dumb,
pleasing the masters, shuffling your feet,

87

answering, "Yes, Massa," to every white man,
learning slave words, how to hold your tongue,
earning no wages for work you had done,
never at liberty to go or to come—
what were your thoughts when you dared not speak?

As time went by all the masters lived freely
with a hypocrisy that dehumanized you.
All was well, for them, with the order of day;
and then an outcry, or expediency,
brought about change, although things stayed the same—
change came in form, not in point of view:
one type of shackle for another kind of chain,
and the "slave masters" went on the same way!

PART 2

There was a proclamation one day;
it was a lot of hullabaloo!
"Freedom," they said, "all you slaves are now free!"
They called it "freedom," sent you on your way
saying you had equal rights from that day;
but you were too quick to think that was true
and that the shackles had melted away.
How you were duped is no mystery.

Chains of the body, chains of the mind,
whichever one, they both are the same.
One is more visible and eats at the body,
The other's more subtle but still has a bind;
though you scarce recognize it, it exists,
it is implanted inside of your brain,
influencing your actions and will to resist—
"Think like a slave and that's all you will be!"

Thus, you were programmed to hate your own kind,
made to believe you were nothing at all,
told that your blackness was ugly, unclean,
given a mythical tail they couldn't find,
you were not human, but something deformed!
They painted pictures of you on the wall,
held everything black in ridicule and scorn,

painted your features grotesque and obscene.

They even invented something called "IQ,"
said you were too dumb to learn anything,
you were an ape, they said, or something gross.
In fact they made you invisible, too!
You were a shadow, a token, a ghost;
you were a "nigger," a shiftless being;
you were "inferior" to them, they would boast,
and you believed it and scorned yourself most!

Soon the conditions were just like before,
though called a "freedman" you could not vote,
you were not free to go where you chose,
you had to heed signs on every door
in public places wherever you went:
"This here's for whites only, niggers keep out!"
Even your money could not be well spent
if it meant breaking the "iron-clad codes"!

Hating yourself then for being born black,
you tried to be something else that you're not,
you tried to straighten your "kinky" hair,
emulate whiteness, pretend you're not black,
you tried to be like the "master" you served,
dress in his image and quickly adopt
his ways till you and his image were merged—
and your identity disappeared!

Now, the slave masters, they knew quite well
if you disliked your own black skin
and you strove hard to be white just like them,
you'd be too busy in your private hell
trying to be something you cannot be,
blaming yourself for the state you are in
rather than struggle against them to be free
from the slavery of brainwashed black men!

PART 3

So you continued as second class,
last to be hired and first one to go,
always in debt, living hand-to-mouth,
paid meager wages for the most menial tasks,
forced into ghettos, shoved to the rear,
having so little and nothing to show,
you were so brainwashed you seemed not to care
and kept on dodging yourself and the truth.

Then like the thunder out of nowhere
echoed strong voices exhorting black men.
"Open your eyes," they said, "cast off your chains,
rid yourselves of false images and false fear,
stand up with dignity, control your destiny,
take a good look at yourselves again,
in your blackness there is true beauty,
in your black blood there are precious strains!"

Then your eyes opened, opened at last!
You saw the shackles controlling your mind;
you saw the evil in every taboo;
you saw the myths of the terrible past;
you saw the falseness in donning another's image;
you saw your blackness for the very first time:
a symbol of pride and a rich heritage,
and in your bosom, you felt freedom too!

It was a feeling like linking again
with the long-severed umbilical cord,
it was like reaching into the past,
back into space, into darkness and then
making contact with a part of your soul!
It was a beautiful thing; there's no word
that can express how it feels to be whole,
to be in tune with your heritage at last—

never again to let shackles return,
never again to be helplessly slaughtered,
never again to surrender your birthright,
never again to be trampled and spurned,
never again to be brainwashed by oppressors,
but with your psyche and soul transfigured,
to walk on God's earth as did your ancestors,
free, with your pride glowing in the sunlight!

## MS in a Bottle
(1972)

I think I'm going to write a letter
which I will place inside a bottle—
a manuscript in a bottle—
about our world and things I've seen.
I'll seal it, and I'll set it on
an ocean that flows throughout time!

Then if someone in a future time
should chance upon my manuscript,
I hope the world is different then.
I hope there are no boundaries,
no barriers of any kind
to separate humanity!

No guarded borders on the earth,
no states or countries to fight for,
no wars, no treaties, armies, guns,
no segregated neighborhoods,
no social classes, poverty,
no racial biases or codes!

Perhaps people will call themselves
brothers and sisters too, at last,
and trust will be a way of life,
and hate will be a word removed
from all the dictionaries,
and from the human heart!

If someone in some future time
should find my bottled manuscript,
perhaps they should not read it, though,
for, reading it they might be shocked
to know what kind of people lived,
hated and killed each other so,
a long, long time ago!

## Children of the Darker Race
(1972)

Speak, O children of the darker race,
brothers and sisters of a sacred past,
speak in your familiar strains
and phrases—music to the ears!
Those treasured themes that you relate
connect the future to the past
and meaning to the present give!

Speak, O brothers and sisters, speak,
speak to the soul's most quiet place
and waken songs long dormant there;
speak to the heart languishing for
knowledge of self and truths about
the realm whence our collective sprang;
speak to the mind, that window, no,
that door that often shuts and keeps
us from our true inheritance!

O speak that those who went before
may hear the music of your voices,
may hear the swelling decibels
that say to them they're not forgotten,
that say we are because they were,
that all we are and do and feel
are the result, fulfillment of
their sacrifices,
as they, too, were for those before them
and those to come shall be for us.
We are one people drawing from
one source, building from one foundation,
the sum of whose parts is equal to
the whole, and this likewise is true:
a tree bears fruit,
no fruit can be without its tree,
it owes its value to its source;
yet each fruit generates a tree
and, thus, a forest grows!

O brothers and sisters, speak
that we shall never dim
the torch our forebears gave to us;
speak that the spirits of our parents,
our parents' parents, our ancestors,
wherever they may be,
may smile on us and know
that all that they endured
was not endured in vain!

Speak, O children of the darker race
though scattered far across the earth,
your own story, your legacy,
was written in blood, and sweat and tears.
The caravan of the fallen
extends throughout eternity.
What price you've paid for your greatness,
greatness predating Christendom, spanning
the chasm of time even beyond the pyramids,
even beyond the flood, to the beginning
of life upon the earth!

O speak and know that in you flows
The blood of warriors, builders, dreamers,
the blood of ancient kings and queens,
the blood of wise and gifted men and women,
the blood of prophets and of saints!
In some far distant time, before the yoke
was placed about your necks,
before the chains and slaver's whip,
you ruled the world and gave mankind true wisdom.
Unblemished time bears witness to your greatness!

So speak, O children of the darker race,
and let the quiet places be not quiet anymore,
let the forgotten be not forgotten,
let every door that kept you from
your true inheritance be opened wide
and never more be closed!

**I Am a Dreamer**
(1972)

I am a dreamer,
a dreamer of justice and human rights,
a dreamer of righting wrongs,
and I was dreaming,
what if the world were color-blind
and the myth of race were no more?
Would the world be one big "kumbaya"
where we loved each other as oneself?
Or would we still discriminate?
Would we still hate and segregate?
What would it be like if no more
we called each other black or white
and all of us looked just alike?
It could not be that pigment then—
or lack of it—would seal our fate.
But since I know the ways of men,
they'd find a way to discriminate.
Yes, some other irrationality
besides judging one by one's skin
instead of by one's character
would be the new absurdity
to drive the "hate" machinery.
It's sad that I should think this way—
but I still hope for a better day.
That's why I am a dreamer.

## Prison Walls
(1977)

"Prison walls are made of skin,"
some say, "and cannot be erased;
depending on which skin you're in,
it's hell you're bound to face!"

But I believe we brand the skin
only because it's there;
real prison walls lie deep within,
they're made of *hate* and *fear*.

How many prisoners are there?
Why, all of us! You see,
we never even bother
to see that we're not free!

We live in our prisons,
don't even mind the cold,
and make up many reasons
to barricade the soul.

So many years of hating
have left a trail of shame,
of senseless human wasting
in this Republic's name.

Yet we go on pretending
that some of us are free,
and keep the caldrons boiling
with hate for you and me.

It isn't any wonder
jails flourish in our time
when you and I surrender
to one another's crime!

We made our prisons very strong,
yet it is not too late
to break the walls and shackles down
and rid the world of hate.

Tear down your jail, earth brother,
and help me tear down mine!
Let us free one another
and wipe the slate of time!

## This Is My Song

We marvel at the same blue sky,
the same bright stars,
the same universe;

we breathe in and out the same air,
drink the same water,
tread the same earth;

we share the same sunlight,
hear the same thunder,
see the same rainbows;

we dream dreams and have the same hopes,
feel the same needs,
the same joys and sorrows;

we are driven by the same fears,
the same thirsts,
the same longings;

we wonder where we came from,
why we are here,
where we are going;

we pray to the same God,
rest when weary,
and soon we are gone!

What is it then that makes us different,
if we are different
as we always claim?

Or is it that we are the same,
though we are different?
I cannot explain.

Am I not like you? Are you not like me?
What do you see
when you look at me?

We are reflections of each other,
manifested only
if we choose to see!

The spirits and souls of all of us,
when we think of it,
have the same destiny.

So why does that not make us brothers
and sisters since we
all came from the same tree?

# Along the Way Poems

## Frightened Men

I've never seen a fretful ant,
a lazy bird, a jilted bee,
a moping squirrel in a tree,
a schizophrenic elephant,

a cow that thinks it isn't a cow,
a fish unhappy with the sea,
a cat that doesn't want to be
and even hates its own meow!

But I've seen frightened men who chase
the phantoms of their discontent,
who court neuroses they invent
to spread among the human race!

## The Mask

We wear a mask wherever we go,
and only we and the mirror know
who dwells behind the mask we wear
and what secrets are hidden there.

I tried to read your mask, and you
were scrutinizing my mask, too.
We thought we knew each other well,
but there are things a mask won't tell.

O what vane images we bring,
pretending and pretending,
while desperately we try to hide
what we are really like inside!

## On the Occasion of a Multiple Death by Fire —1

There was no heat; the rooms were damp and cold.
They begged and begged, "Please give us heat tonight!"
The landlord scowled and scorned their helpless plight
demanding extra rent he said they owed—
his Shylock greed all but consumed his soul!
No flesh and blood should shiver through the night
while heat is hoarded out of greed and spite,

for human lives are worth much more than gold.

They had no heat and lit a faulty heater.
The room was cold—what else could they have done?
They went to sleep then, tempting death by fire
that blistering night, that cold night in December;
and when the early morning light had come,
they were enveloped in a burning pyre.

## On the Occasion of a Multiple Death by Fire—2

Engulfed by flames she frightfully awoke.
"Lord, give me strength to save my family!"
She threw her children one by one to safety
returning each time through the fire and smoke,
then from the window desperately she spoke,
"Take care of them, take care of them for me!"
and disappeared into the burning sea
that rose so fast it soon was at her throat.

Those on the higher floor were trapped inside
still sleeping. And they'll never wake again.
It must have been for them that she returned.
She and her relatives all sadly died
and left behind four helpless little children
orphaned the night their heatless flat had burned.

## The Beggar

"Mister, can you spare some change?
Madam, can you help me please?"
Those words rang out in the morning air
as a mass of rushing, trampling feet
in reckless rhythm hurried by
past the beggar with cup in hand!
Thousands went by in the morning air
with nary a glance, with nary a sigh,
like a horde of creatures in the wilds
with steel-like stares so cold and grim,
with trampling feet in the morning air.

"Mister, can you spare some change?
Madam, can you help me please?"
It seemed that no one heard nor cared,
though the words rang out in the morning air.
On they passed, hundreds, thousands passed
and I guess there were times, few and far between,
when a *clink* was heard above the din,
and a "God bless you, Sir," or "God bless you, Ma'am"!
But who knows how many beggars there are
at this very moment in the whole wide world,
standing by some roadside with cup in hand
while a sea of humanity goes passing by?
And who knows how many cups in hand,
how many "God bless you" have gone by,
how many beggars have come and gone—
and why—since the world began?

**Bar Room Orgy**
(1972)

The room was dimly lit with varicolored lights
like Chinese lanterns hanging from the ceiling;
and leaning against the counter
on their cushioned swivel seats,
a dozen patrons sat with glasses in their hands.
In a corner on a platform
the fat man stomped the floor,
a-one... a-two... a-one...a-two...
The bongo player picked up the time
and rapped his knuckles out trying
to keep up with the drummer and
piano player too.
The singer, microphone in hand,
waited until he got a cue
then "Yeh, yeh, yeh," he blasted,
straining his vocal chords,
"Yeh, yeh, yeh, wheeeeeeee, I got mine,"
and on and on he sang.
Then in a psychedelic whirl
the whole band scintillated
to a rhythmical crescendo!
With perspiration dripping down,
with shirt necks open, heads flinging,
the band got down:
A-one...a-two...a-one...a-two...
Ra-ta-ta-ta-tat-a-tat,
R-r-r-r-ron con co con co con co con,
ta ra ta ra ta ra ta ra,
"Yeh, yeh, yeh, wheeeeeeee,
I got mine,"
and on and on it went!
The platform shook. The room
was flooded with the sounds
as patrons gulped their spirits down
and asked for more refills.
One lady turned and shook her head
and shoulders with the music;

'twas hard to tell if music or the booze
was taking over then.  Another patron
jumped to his feet, started to jig and turn.

More heads began swaying in the room,
fingers were popping, glasses tinkling,
the singer with his "Yeh, yeh, yeh,"
bent over backward, hands in the air.
Oh the music got so hot then:
a-one...a-two...a-one...a-two...
a ra-ta-ta-ta-tat-, ta tat ta tat,
r-r-r-r-r-ron con co co con con co con,
ta ra ta ra ta ra,
"Wheeeeeeee, I got mine!"
More patrons on the floor whining, turning;
the booze was flowing high and fast,
even the barmaid started to twist,
to serve and twist, to twist and serve.
One man with glassy eyes (You knew
it wasn't the music turned him on.)
gave out a yell "Whoooooppppeeeeeeee"
and rolled out on the floor,
then picked himself up "whoooppeeeing"
as the strange cacophony rang down the rafters,
a-one, a-two, a-one, a-two,
a ra-ta-tat-a-tat-a-tat-a-tat,
ron con co con co con co con,
ree pleet, ree pleet, ta-ra-ta-ra pleet,
"Yeah, yeh, yeh, wheeeeeeee, I got mine,
whhhooooooopppeeeeeeeee!"
And as I sat watching this frenzied orgy,
I suddenly asked myself,
Lord, what am I doing here?

**When New Yorkers Are Safely Locked in for the Night**
(1978)

When New Yorkers are safely locked in for the night
and shadows conceal alley cats out of sight,
when Wall Street looks like a graveyard zone,
and Delancey and Court Streets' hustle-bustle is gone,
when Broadway playhouses have closed for the night
and Lincoln Center crowds have taken flight,
when most shops and stores are closed in the city,
when the usually hectic Port Authority
and Penn Station bustle comes to a hush
and the booths are shut down till the morning rush,
when the subways, if running, are far in between,
and the night air and darkness envelope the scene,
when the hour's between midnight and twilight of morning,
when the good citizens lie in their beds snoring,
a world of the living dead reigns supreme,
a world of the wretched, the damned, the cast-offs,
the hopelessly tainted, the wasted, the lost,
the desperate, the broken in spirit and mind,
an anti- or sub-world of yours and mine,
a world of creatures cuddled in corners in the cold,
sprawled on benches, or creeping, crawling out from some
hole,
a world of empty glances, of pitiful stares,
of haggard looks and of raggedy wares,
of swollen and often of rotting flesh,
a world of zombies with the smell of dead fish
roaming in the night air, in a bottomless pit
where the lower the level, a level is beneath it,
a world of lost souls ghoulishly surviving,
being victims more than victimizing,
a world where all Christian laws are dead,
where the laws are the laws of the jungle instead,
a world where human values do not count,
where up is down and down is out,
a world with its codes that are different from ours,
where the fear's not of darkness but of daylight hours,
a world wherein kindness is an ugly word,
where a gift is suspicious and a giver absurd,
where brutality itself seems a generous thing

109

if instead of being maimed the victim stops breathing.

When busy New Yorkers' workday is done
and they sleep, most of them snuggly bedded down,
the guilt of humanity cannot sleep,
the guilt of humanity is walking the street,
up and down Time Square, Forty-Second Street,
Eighth Avenue, Broadway, the Port Authority beat,
Penn Station, the West Side, the East Side, along the
Square,
Harlem, uptown, downtown, everywhere,
flaking, flicking, tricking, cruising along,
snorting, shooting whatever they get their hands on,
aimless, mindless, without feeling or fears,
groping, scratching, dying, and nobody cares,
killing, stealing, shooting junk in their veins
in the bottomless pit where the living dead reign.

When New Yorkers are safely locked in for the night
and shadows conceal alley cats out of sight,
the guilt of humanity cannot sleep,
the guilt of humanity is walking the street...

## There Are Parallels in Everything

As I sat musing over the day's events,
citing the wrongs committed, and deeds too,
I stole myself away for one brief moment,
and, with no thought of what was to ensue,
brought all my strength to bear in one swift blow
of my clenched fist upon a table top;
slowly, in pain, and with a deep remorse
inside that I cannot explain somehow,
I raised my lethal fist from off the spot.
Gone was the pain, I cured it with a curse!

But on the table top there lay an ant
whose lifeless figure, smashed, whose minute brain
was pulp-like now, and I could not supplant
my guilt real or imagined, or my disdain!
Maybe it was symbolic but, no less,
a victim of my predatory whim
that uncomplaining ant I sent speeding
into the infamy of timelessness
without a prayer, torn now from limb to limb...
yet, there are parallels in everything!

One day like all creatures, undoubtedly,
we, too, must mingle with the elements.
And when that time comes, will we go swiftly,
dispatched by some blind act of violence?
I read about a manmade bomb today
more lethal than my fists could ever be.
It was dropped on a city far away
and pulverized thousands upon thousands
of innocent souls of humanity.
O Lord, how great a guilt to bear is man's?

## A-woe A-wee

O weep you skies! O wild winds blow!
Instead of snow
let torrents pour
a-weeping and a-moaning,
how came we to this Jersey shore
on a stormy Saturday morning?
I remember now,
I had lost my mind
and was chasing a rainbow
hoping to find
amidst glitter and glare
a pot of gold down here.

I chased all the way
on the parkway
the rainbow in my mind,
only to find
there's no pot of gold down here,
anywhere,
only slick leprechauns
luring you on,
turning your head
with tricks, illusions,
treats and delusions
to steal your gold instead.

A-woe a-wee, what a bitter day,
this stormy Saturday morning.
I can't tell which is worse, this day
or the way that I am feeling;
but the truth is so revealing:
To journey this far
where, indeed, phantoms are
and become victim is appalling.
Eagerly we come
to be undone
by the sounds of sirens calling,
by sweet sounds of sirens calling.

Even the stormy winds that blow
give every hint of warning

to the wise, "No, no, do not go
where the luckless are all swarming
and the price you'll pay is alarming.
O wise winds, blow, blow, blow.
How could we not know
when the signs were there portending?
But the blind won't see, and the deaf can't hear
while sweet sounds of sirens are calling,
"Come to our lair, come to our lair,"
ever so enthralling.

If you want good advice
let this suffice,
and it will never fail you:
Build your hopes and dreams
on what's real, tried and true
works for you, simple as it seems.
In a den built on schemes
there can be no silver lining.
Just one rule applies to the victims:
those who build schemes
based on human beings sinning
are the only ones who end up winning.

A-woe a-wee, a-woe a-wee,
what a bitter Saturday morning.

## I Never Walk Alone

I never walk alone while I share human sorrow
or joy that leaves its mark. Each human contact touches
me:
Something is given, something gained with every chance
encounter.
I join in human gladness not by choice, in spite of it—
how can I walk alone?
I share a victory with each heart that sings
and turn from gloom with every human smile.
Each kindness has a way to move me;
though someone else receives it, yet I feel
the warmth as if I were receiving,
or were the giver with a heart of gold.
This life is mixed with grief as well as gladness,
like vintage that is bittersweet—
none shall escape who shares the human circumstance.
Today we live; each day we die a little when our fellow
man
falls by the wayside, victim of the yoke that binds us all,
for no one dies alone.
I never walk alone; a crowd's beside me: voices touching
mine,
cries in the wilderness echoing mine, a need that is my
need,
a hope that is my hope multiplied all around me,
keeping me company.
And so, no matter where I am I shall go forth, my hand in
hand
with all brothers beneath the skin—
to meet with destiny.

# Autumn Poems

## To Autumn

O autumn, latter time of year,
precursor of drear, frosty days,
unlike summer you do not wear
lush greenery, nor are your ways

like summer's—she draws crowds to play
in parks and fields during her stay,
but you with gustier breath, you may
just chase children of summer away.

It must make you somewhat sad, too,
that people seem to want to run
or quicken stride because of you,
when you just wish they'd have some fun

and stay awhile to get a hug,
or some friendly exchange, but not
a hasty cover up and shrug.
What must you do to change such lot?

O autumn, be not dismayed at all;
you're not like summer, yet be content
for you have talents, too, after all.
Long after summer has been spent,

your trees and leaves turn gold and red,
purple and brown, brighter than a rainbow
that adorns the skies when storms are sped!
O autumn, your displays are so

Enchanting, no artist could paint
a better masterpiece than you;
such warmth is captured and contained
in every color, in every hue,

and travelers stop while on their way
to marvel at your gorgeous scene
that is, for me, in every way
among the loveliest I have seen.

To show how much you, too, are loved,

your picture postcards are everywhere;
paintings of you hang in the Louvre,
and are admired throughout the year.

So envy not your sister clime,
youth has its assets, that is true;
but in the course of passing time,
maturity has beauty, too!

**Too Soon a Rose Must Die**

Too soon a rose must die—
and leave no vestige of its charms
to greet the open sky
and deck the autumn scene!

Too soon shall winter usher in
and cover with its mantle white
the hills and fields of green
where summer joys had been!

Too soon the fiddler's tune plays out
and sings no more
what yesterday was all about
when it is gone!

Too soon—yet swift as time may go,
there's still a little while to share
and songs to sow
before the shade must come!

## If I Were a Poet

If I were a poet, I couldn't help but show it,
for I'd paint many colors in rhyme;
I'd rhyme a rainbow, just as you see it,
to last a long, long time.

If I were a poet, you'd certainly know it,
for I'd set down into rhyme
a rose so resplendent that naught could undo it,
not even the passage of time.

If I were a poet, my very next sonnet
would be a robin's song
whose joy ever fleeting would live, once I've penned it,
after the robin is gone!

If I were a poet, I'd capture the spirit
of an eagle in its flight.
Such splendor—my verses would always display it
though the eagle had vanished from sight!

If I were a poet, I'd capture a comet
as it went streaking by
over the purple silhouette
of mountains against the sky.

If I were a poet, I'd bring home the sunset
that floods the evening sky;
the warmth of that moment when we reveled in it
would never, never die!

## It Is a Lonely Sight to See

It is a lonely sight to see
naked branches on a tree,
when it was not that long ago
there were so many leaves to show.

Trees all around were thick and green
and sheltered many nests unseen!
Branches stretched far with leaves thereon
all reaching out to kiss the sun!

Now, where did all the green leaves go
and all the friends we used to know?
There were so many long ago
before autumn and threat of snow!

Most have now fallen to the ground
like leaves of autumn, one by one;
yet but a few cling to the tree,
waiting and wondering patiently.

## Autumn Leaves

Autumn, Autumn, your leaves are falling.
When news comes now it is to say,
sadly another leaf has fallen
from off the tree of life today.

There was a time news used to be
about who's dating whom, or where
is going to be the next house party,
or what's the latest thing to wear.

And nothing would be more newsworthy
than who is getting married to whom,
or, save your best outfit, get ready
for the hottest dance that's coming soon.

And always news about the families,
that everyone was doing fine,
would fill discourse with pleasantries
and make sweeter the fruit of the vine.

Yes, when such good news came already
we were so glad to hear and share,
like who graduated summa cum laude
or who gave birth to twins this year.

Then all the news began to change
and had a different, sadder tone;
that what before might have seemed strange,
now can't be blamed on chance alone

O Autumn, Autumn, it's so unfair.
Bring me no more sad news today.
The tree of life will be too bare
if all the leaves are gone away.

## Autumn's Curse

Autumn must bode the saddest time of year
when all the fertile fields are gleaned and bare,
and all who were once, oh, so young and fair
have felt the measure of life's harvest shear!

Yes, harvest time's a great thing, may be so,
at least for Him who does the harvesting,
when youths, after their years of fun and show,
must face the time of final reckoning.

O autumn, least envied and for these reasons:
you trail behind most glorious spring and summer
and lead into the harshest of all seasons,
the chilly blasts and extreme cold of winter!

Winter, though, unlike you, before it's done,
no matter how severe the cold it brings,
knows when its ice and snow at last are gone,
it gives way to the miracle of spring!

So what have you to say, O kindred autumn,
coming between the brightest and worst?
O season most pensive and all too solemn,
you brood for lost youth—that must be your curse!

# Soul Poems

## The Little Fly

Whenever nighttime settled down
a myriad army gathered round
the street lamps that lit up our town.
They came like curious people from
the fields and shrubberies all around
the outskirts of our little town
and sought the burning orbs of light
that seemed to glitter with delight
on having friends to spend the night.
They formed a whirling train around
the glowing lamplight's searing crown,
all night a mad merry-go-round.
Sometimes they crashed into their sun
as I had stood for hours by
watching them with a boy's keen eye.
And if one stalwart little fly,
wounded, fell from its orbit high,
my joy for it unbounded grew
when it had darted up anew
its dizzying orbit to renew.
Today when life's setbacks call,
if I should have a sudden fall,
instead of lying by some wall
and trying not to rise at all,
I think about the little fly
that flashes on my inner eye
and rise again to my orbit high.

## I Think Music's a Blessing

Only unfettered thoughts so pure
flow freely through the mind
when, in my room, music's rapture
floats from the Grundig's pine.

The colorful tones are liquid pure
like cleansing mountain streams
that from rich fountains gaily pour
their smooth and languid themes.

They are like moon glow shining on
a quiet, fresh, green valley glade
to glimmer in a glassy pond
where water lilies wade.

The swirling tones are sweet like wine
the best vintage had made;
they dance out from the Grundig's pine
and whirl about, then fade;

but soon new mixtures usher out
and fill the air once more—
a marching train goes round about
and swells just as before.

You almost can reach out and touch
the sea of tones that float,
and make your hand just like a cup
and drink up every note!

The jeweled tones sparkle like gems
in a glittering cavalcade,
and a multi-magic lightness sends
you in their sea to wade.

I think music's a blessing
for it will never cease
(though strife can be distracting
and other pleasures please)

to join the mind to spheres above,
the spirit to its fountainhead,
the heart to universal love,
the soul to angels where angels tread!

## Wishing

I once wished I could climb the tallest tree,
defying gravity.
I wished that I could scale a wall
that was too tall.
I wished that I could ride a bull—
that seemed so cool!
I even wished that I could fly
but had the good sense not to try.
O what a wishful fool I have been,
the biggest one you've ever seen.
If God wanted me to climb trees,
He'd give me claws like squirrels and monkeys.
If He wanted me to scale a wall,
He'd give me sticky feet so I wouldn't fall;
and if He wanted me to fly,
He'd give me wings like a butterfly.

I once wished that I was very tall,
but thought it too cramped at ten feet tall
if I had to fit into a space too small.
Once I even wished to be a clown
with masquerade and a funny frown;
but sooner than later life taught me
not to count on wishes too much, you see,
wishing won't help me get out of a jam
if I don't even trust who and what I am.
There's a reason God made us the way we are
and gave us enough to be thankful for
instead of wishing for this or that
and letting our whole life go to pot.

I guess if we trusted in God's design
we'd be thankful for every detail we find
just the way He made it, His purpose divine,
and we'd be happy he even had us in mind.
Nevertheless I guess it's a human thing,
this weakness that is not too unforgiving,
that sometimes we still find ourselves wishing.

## Memories

Priceless souvenirs that grip and bind,
turning inward our heart and mind;
empty cups that once held vintage wine;
vanished sights and scenes revisited
in old pictures where they're locked in time;

gifts now faded yet that still remain
fresh as kisses cold kindled again;
stories shared when meeting an old friend;
dim reflections dancing in a pool
where time's ripples undulate with them;

songs we used to hear and loved to sing
when our world was just beginning;
sounds of far off voices echoing
through the corridors of space and time--
ancient laughter sweet returning;

quiet places, lovers' rendezvous;
monograms on barks of trees we knew;
broken dolls gathering dust and mildew;
letters written, oh, so long ago;
promises too many or too few;

shadows, forms and shapes now barely seen;
faces faintly focused on a screen;
friendships drifted or that time has weaned;
deeds long past that helped to shape our lives;
kindness from a stranger not since seen;

trophies on a wall, bright victories;
pleasures from across the misty seas;
pain and sorrow too, yes, all of these,
that the heart and inward mind perceive,
are the soul's eternal memories!

### The Diggers Burial Ground

Here is the diggers hallowed burial ground,
the place where fallen silver workers sleep,
here on a crowded hill that's not so steep,
dampened by rain, warmed by the tropic sun!
Walk you there with a deep reverence among
the stones and take great care lest trampling feet
should disrespect these honored dead, who sleep
within the earth now that their toil is done!

It's well that we should reverence where they're laid,
these countless bright and brave women and men,
who gained so little and who so much gave,
who braved forces the faint-hearted would dread;
and though the world tries hard now to forget them,
let us not tread harshly upon their graves!

## O Land Where My Father Labored and Died

O Land where my father labored and died
and where my mother lies now by his side,
both sleeping on a very quiet hillside
where many sons and daughters there abide;

O Land that once divided two oceans
until bold and relentless excavations
gouged out your stubborn mountainsides,
stirring your wrath that unleashed bitter landslides;

O Land where brave Caribbeans once stood
and toiled and sacrificed their precious blood
so that two mighty oceans then could meet
and many nations prosper at your feet;

O Land of my birth where long, long ago
countless dramas played out, and life springs flowed
from so many brave men and women although
the world acknowledged not—nor cared to know;

O Land that has taken and given in return,
whose gifts to man our forebears more than earned
and paid for drop by drop while being spurned
and cast aside like shoes grown old and worn;

O land, where is there justice? Is there none
for them who toiled here and who now are gone?
They were not even welcomed at the feast
after they gave the most and gained the least.

O land, unblinded justice, where is such?
If you should know, tell me it's not too much
to ask why on this grassy, ill-kept hillside
our fathers' graves are strewn carelessly aside

till even weeds gain more respect and flourish
while covering o'er the graves of those we cherish?
Here on this open, soggy field, it's hard to find
even a name or stone of any kind.

O tell me that we owe them more than this!
The silent voices of the dead insist,
"Forget us not here now among these weeds
that are degrading to our lives and past deeds.

If we meant anything, if there was worth
in our struggles once upon the earth,
forget us not and cast us not aside
as if we never strived hard ere we died."

I glance now at this field of fallen men
and women whose kind we'll never see again,
this remnant of the silvermen who came
from far across the seas and helped to tame

a jungle, brave its hazardous terrain,
carve out its mountainsides in sun and rain
at the highest cost of blood and human pain—
and wonder, did they sacrifice in vain?

Is this the thanks then, that we give to them,
to lie unhallowed, neglected, and condemned
to the ravages of soggy grass and weeds,
forgotten like forgotten debts and deeds?

O land where brave Caribbeans once stood
and toiled and sacrificed their precious blood,
if not for them who paved for us the way
where would we be, where would we be today?

O land, in name of justice and respect,
However long before it takes effect,
cry out, cry out to all humanity
to treat this resting place with dignity!

## O Land of Promise

O land of promise, land of tropic splendor,
lifting up girders and new towers each day!
O booming city perched beside a bay,
rising, perhaps too fast, above the shore
while needs are being neglected at your core!
Your wealth lifts not places in disarray
and broken lives that struggle everyday
in poverty with little hope of more.

O Nation, think of whence your blessings came
and those upon whose bones today you stand
who planted here the seeds from which you thrive.
What would you reap if things had stayed the same
and there was no canal flowing through this land?
Then share the wealth that others, too, may live!

## The House on Lafayette Avenue

There was a time not long ago
when all roads seemed to lead you there
to that three-story house, even so,
people would come from everywhere;
some found their way there through the years
seeking help and encouragement
while passing through—mostly young adults
facing a harsh predicament,
studying and struggling to make their way
with just a dream, sometimes no clue!
Thank heavens for them they came there
to the house on Lafayette Avenue,
to the right place and the right people
who were only too happy to show them the way
and help them through rough times they would meet,
providing them a place to stay
until they could get back on their feet.

For how many people through the years
the house on Lafayette Avenue
played a part in their lives and careers?
And how many people have broken bread there
or said a prayer and shared good cheers?
Something was special at that address!
Maybe the magic was simply this:
the house on Lafayette Avenue was blessed,
and the blessings that dwelled inside that home
were the goodness and charity of one Aunt Ness
and her dear Sam, her quiet champion!

If you ever knew Anesta and Sam
and spent an evening at their home;
if you ever chatted with them awhile
and heard them in their humble tone
speak of their values and beliefs,
how just by helping others alone
brought them joy and fulfillment;
if you ever visited them any evening
notwithstanding a crowd, which was not surprising
(whether or not it was a special event
or a meeting or just friends socializing),

you would feel their genuine love and warmth,
you would know their generous hospitality,
and why the house on Lafayette Avenue
was a special place, a second home to many;
why struggling young people, too many to mention,
did well in life after staying there;
why so many friends came from far away, too,
to meet and to share rich memories there;
and you'd know why a name written on that avenue
is the name *S. Anesta Samuel*.

Now both Anesta and Sam are gone.
And there are no more gatherings there today
at two-seventy-six Lafayette Avenue,
Brooklyn, New York, U. S. A.;
but if you should ever pass that way
and look at the street sign and the house that is near,
give pause for a moment before you walk away,
and pay a tribute to the couple who once lived there,
and the lives made better because they were here!

## Old Truths, Old Faiths, Old Friends

When through the years I've strayed away from you,
not so intending but to face the world
seeking my fortune with brash wings unfurled,
and, in my straying, memories overdue
were pushed aside by things not half so true;
when games, when phantoms and pursuits absurd
contrived only to make my vision blurred
and I groped in a place I hardly knew,
deceiving self, giving false values to
misshapen things and hollow victories,
some wondrous thing, such as a childhood song
a stranger sings that echoes through and through,
bursts all the floodgates of my memories
and brings me back to where I started from.

## A Life Never Lived

A hand never shaken—
a voice never heard—
a choice never taken—
a world undiscovered—

a joy not partaken—
a song never uttered—
a love un-awakened—
a door barred and shuttered—

a mind never nourished—
a soul never grieved—
a heart never cherished—
a life never lived!

**Little Girl**
(Dedicated to my niece, Sonya Evans, when she
was five years old)


Little girl, little girl,
with your dimples and your curls,
with your childish innocence
(Fragile armor of defense!),
how eager you are to grasp
things grownups ignore at last,
but a child will never pass!

Little girl, little girl,
with your dimples and your curls,
with your two bright eyes afire
like the stars that I admire,
and your two frail little hands
touching everything that stands,
you're a joy, that's what you are,
more than any little star!

Little girl, little girl,
with your dimples and your curls,
how you spread such happiness
with your pretty little face
like a prayer in its place!
You pretend you're worldly, though
there is so much you don't know;
but until the day you do,
it will never bother you!

Little girl, little girl,
with your dimples and your curls,
you are like a parakeet,
everything your lips repeat!
I have wondered if you knew
whether what you said was true!
You are cheerful all day long,
while grownups worry and frown;
you must think the world is one
big, happy merry-go-round.

Little girl, little girl,
with your dimples and your curls,
with your gift for make believe,
what strange tales sometimes you weave!
How your playthings lie around
you scattered upon the ground,
speaking to you in their tongue!
There are dolls and dishes, cups—
they'll be real when you grow up!

Little girl, little girl,
with your dimples and your curls,
when your playful hours are sped
how you lie upon your bed
like an angel, so blessed,
off to fairyland to dream
of sugar, spices, and ice cream
and sights such as you've never seen!

Little girl, little girl,
with your dimples and your curls,
what, I wonder, will become
of you when play days are gone
and childhood's a long-hushed song.
Heaven help you then, I pray,
teach you how to find your way!

## Lost Innocence

Speak dearly of another day,
another world, another place,
where different medleys filled the air
and life's truths had a different taste.

Speak fondly of another day,
of fledgling pursuits of long ago
when such adventures were so sweet
and there were no regrets to know.

Speak kindly of another day
when dreams and dreaming gave us wings,
and every day's imaginings
were filled with new and wondrous things.

Speak softly of another day,
of lost joy, treasures of yesteryear
that Time has weaned or swept away
and left only an echo here.

Speak gently of another time,
another rhythm, another rhyme,
when immortality sublime
was seen through eyes that were once mine.

Speak, speak, O Shadow, of another time,
the only time we'll ever know
when beauty held full sway, and when
death had no sting—and life no woe.

Speak, speak, O Shadow, dark was that day,
that day the fruit of knowledge gave
our earthly paradise away
when it burst on the lips of Eve!

**She Was Like A Flower Sweet And Bright**
(Dedicated to Mola Alphonse)

She was like a flower sweet and bright,
with a cheerful heart and a joyful smile;
she was like a flower sweet and bright,
only here for just a little while!

She was born on an island in the sun
and was raised full of pride and a generous love;
she was born where the heart throbbed with nature as one,
and the soul with the sea and the heavens above.

She was blessed with a kind of heavenly grace
and a childish mischief oft' misunderstood;
there was always a kindness in her face
and an eagerness in her to do good.

She left home, left her island in the sun
in the prime of her youth for a land far away,
taking with her the truths of the world she was from
and a faith that would guide her through life, come what
may.

There was hope in her heart to fulfill her life's plan
in a country that seemed so strange yet so grand.
But one day in that strange and distant land,
like a flower, she was crushed by a violent hand.

She was like a flower sweet and bright
with a cheerful heart and a joyful smile;
she was like a flower sweet and bright
that bloomed on this earth for a little while.

## Shopper's Christmas

Once more that latter time of year is here,
marked with its show of greetings and good cheers,
when carols seem to frown on human tears
and we forget the burdens that we bear.
Once more the toys and glitter reappear,
and all the stores rush to display their wares
while frenzied shoppers plunge with reckless gears
into debt's chasm on a buying tear.

They say it is a birth they celebrate
while trampling o'er each other in the aisles,
and as the hour closes in on them,
their frenzy mounts that it may be too late
for one more plunge, for one more debtor's prize
before the season goes away again.

**A Frightened Little Bird**
(An encounter that happened in my classroom
in my second year of teaching at
La Boca, C.Z. Elementary School in 1954.)

One day a frightened little bird
into a room had made its way—
by what mistake it had entered
has puzzled me up to this day!

The doors were locked till I came in;
windows were shut, and all around,
no opening large enough for him
to force his entrance could be found!

Fiercely against a wire screen
high on a wall it threw its weight
repeatedly as I, unseen,
resolved to tip the scales of fate.

How long it struggled there in vain
to gain its freedom once again
I knew not; but exhaustion claimed
its efforts when it fell in pain!

I knelt and held the little bird
with all the gentleness I could,
while not a nerve within it stirred
as I before a window stood.

I opened wide the window then
and let a gush of air rush in,
which soothed the bird to life again
and made it long to join its kin.

A grateful look beamed in its eye
and touched me with a gladness, too,
as off it flew into the sky
with all its hopes revived anew!

I watched it till its distant flight
had reached the far horizon's arm,

142

when from my feeble mortal sight
heaven had swallowed up its form.

And, silently, somehow I knew
as I had helped a bird that day,
a hand shall lead my footsteps, too,
when I am lost along the way!

**Fellow Traveler**
(Dedicated to Alvin Roy Williams)

O friend, the years you faced life's common foe
your silent fears and mine were much the same!
We struggled in life's crucible; our bane
was being born poor; yet, our bond will show
somehow we helped each other's creed to grow!
We were each other's mirror whence we gained
insights about faith, life, suffering, pain,
and drew courage and hope to counter woe.

We dreaded death but spoke not of it often;
and pushed it, like a bad dream, far away!
Alas, the truth is, it is always near!
So when you lay there quiet in your coffin,
I saw a traveler who had passed this way,
and that he did has made a difference here.

**Alvinroy**
(Dedicated to my friend Alvin Roy Williams)

O wretched Sorrow, shed your bitter tears!
O Melancholy drear, awake and weep!
Arise and summon all of your compeers,
though not to waken from eternal sleep
dear Alvinroy, for he has surely gone
where all men, soon or late, one day must go
when each his destined hour at last has come;
but summon them that they might mourn him who
had made the angels proud before he died.
Though trampled and though mocked in his last days
by pressing Death, he went, unterrified,
as if certain that when the final haze
like clouds had cleared, all would be rectified,
for soulless Death with all his fearful ways
cannot beyond the grave's portals abide!

Come, all you mourners, come, by Sorrow led,
and sing 'midst tears his praise! Who would not choose
to lend a flow of kind words o'er his bed
bidding peace his eternal sleep profuse?
I sing for Alvinroy! How we did drink
youth's nourishment out of the same fountain,
debate so hard sometimes we could not think,
only to find our arguments the same
though our semantics seemed awhile to differ.

How we had sat and played through many a game
of chess and delved through notes and books together
late in the night, both seeking to find truth,
unmindful of the time or state of weather,
but always happy when we found the root
of some great problem through trial and error.

Now, no more shall you play the royal game
you loved, which used to please Caissa's eye,
for you are gone and shall not come again,
O Alvinroy for whom sad mourners cry!
How orphaned dreams stand leaning o'er his coffin
weeping sadly because their precious home
is gone and shall not rise again in him.

145

How Hope now staggers with a woeful moan
to think she nurtured him so tenderly,
and, after all the loving care she gave,
after the endless vigil, finally,
surrendered him by force up to the grave!
It is too hard for her when she must lose
one whom she tried her very best to save—
O Death, why did you not somewhere else choose?

Courage, in black, a pallor in her cheeks,
pauses, shaken, her grief now unrestrained
for him who fought during the closing weeks –
a champion though gripped with inhuman pain.
Knowing full well the great might of his foe,
and knowing, too, the struggle it was lost,
brave Alvinroy clasped Death as he laid low
and gave himself up to the Holy Ghost!

All this Courage had witnessed by his bed,
and in her heart she knew she had no power
to save him once the Reaper's viper head
had made its wound and marked the final hour.
O Courage, weep for him who now is gone,
that such a promise, such a precious flower
shall no more flourish in the radiant sun.

Fate, in the shadows, holds her head bent low,
her shame that she had penned his coming doom
reveals itself upon her wrinkled brow;
that she had played a treacherous part with Gloom
and tireless Death to end a life so fair
tears at her now and will not give her peace,
O would that she could write a different year
upon the eternal slate! The very least,
it would give joy to all his saddened peers
to hear his voice upon this earth again,
to hear his laughter sweet upon their ears,
to see his cheeks flush when joy thereon reigned,
to see him set upon some problem's core
with simple logic and hear him explain—
O we'd rejoice in his wisdom once more!

But Fate and all her armies cannot change now

the finished work of Death once signed and sealed;
despite the tears of vain Regret and Sorrow,
what has been is, and cannot be repealed.
Come, mourners, come Past Joys and Passions cold,
and Winged Desires of another day,
Splendors, Past Deeds, Achievements, Triumphs Old,
sobbing in your sadness and your dismay!
Come, pageantry of old friends, all heartbroken,
in slow procession pass his funeral bier.
Come all, until the last farewells are spoken
under an open sky, then lower him there,
and cover him with earth and flowers gay.
Alas! just one carved stone shall point to where
the clay that once was flesh returns to clay.

O Alvinroy, when Spring returns next year,
her wakened glories and her famous blooms
shall want to know why is it you're not here
to greet them and to sift their sweet perfumes.
What must we say to them when they shall ask,
when Glads and Lilacs greet us, Roses smile
and Morning Glories beckon as we pass?
What shall we say and, saying, not beguile
a host of friends, not only flowers that bloom,
but also flocks that soon will be returning?
Shall we say, in his heart there's no more room
for all the joys that flourish in the spring?
That he has lost interest in Nature's children
and shuns the sight of every flower garden,
or cares not if a robin sings again?

Yet if we said such things they'd surely know,
no matter how convincing we might be,
such words are false and never could be so.
O Alvinroy, they know your heart is worthy
and would not turn from them; so when they ask,
we'll say to them, "His flesh lies in the earth,
but earth cannot contain his spirit dear,
for it is wakened now to untold mirth
in that most glorious realm above earth where
mortality shall have no more rebirth.
So Spring, rejoice for him though he's away,
tell all your children keep sweet memories

of him when in his prime, when bright and gay,
when he was full of dreams and melodies
and was attuned to all your blooms of May."

O Alvinroy, now laid to eternal sleep,
O friend whose spirit now has home returned,
we who remain, our rendezvous to keep,
still strain to comprehend what you have learned,
for now your spirit walks upon the shore
of that blessed kingdom filled with boundless love.
Why do we weep for him? O weep no more!
His soul is joined by angels far above
who see in him their own and who are pleased.
He moves in their society forever
without fearing that joy now shall be ceased.
If tears are shed, shed them for us who linger,
who wrestle with the tides of pain and strife,
who struggle but one day who must surrender
and leave behind the illusions of this life.

## Yet I Cannot Perceive

Why is it such a natural thing, I ask,
that men fear darkness, not the light of day,
except when they indulge sinister play?
Why do they pine if things slip from their grasp,
and hasten change while clinging to the past?
Why do they crave for fruits that soon decay,
or worship beauty that must fade away,
and cling to dreams housed in a dreamlike mask?

So it is true that nothing mortal lasts,
and as I speak this moment, too, is gone.
Yet I cannot perceive a universe
made of such frailties that so soon must pass,
unless mortality is an illusion
caused by some natural cosmic force dispersed.

## The Masterpiece

The Master looked around and said,
"I'm going to make a masterpiece
like no other that was ever made
whose mettle must be strong, at least,
to stand the test of time and will!"
He chose a massive piece of jade
that would test any sculptor's skill,
even one at the top of his trade,
and thus a great venture began
in a workshop with a master plan!

The first strokes—they were deftly made—
while agile hands the carving did,
and from the mass of lifeless jade,
the work began to be fulfilled.
I watched the sculptor as he gauged
the massive, formless, lifeless jade;
I saw him slowly engage
his trustful tool made to abrade
this stubborn jade that would submit
to his will and determined grit.

Bit by bit...strip by strip...
day by day...strip by strip...
the pieces flew as the sculptor dipped
his piercing tool in the curving hip
and thigh along the statue's side.
As more new scraps were carved away,
the sculptor murmured, showing pride,
"Just wait till the appointed day,
when men shall view you. They shall raise
one name to new heights with their praise!"

And with these words the Master's plan
proceeded well year after year,
evolving in the work at hand.
O sculptor, with the utmost care
and years of practice ply your stroke!
"Ambition I can comprehend,

but what magic will you invoke
to separate you from all men?"
He heard me not, and so went on
humming and carving from dusk till dawn!

The progress of this work of art
was very slow, you must admit,
but you could tell it from the start
that great art does not speed permit
as sculpture and sculptor both took shape;
meanwhile piles of green scraps escaped,
and I, in awe, could only gape
at the sculptor while he smoothly scraped
another layer of jaded strips
along the statue's graceful hips.

Slowly the masterpiece evolved
under the workroom's glimmering light,
and any doubt was soon dissolved
in an all-inspiring sight!
The lady's hair stretched long and free
about her neck and shoulders bare;
her face beamed exquisitely
before the mesh of dangling hair!
A smooth and radiant smile she gave
to turn beholder into slave.

Within her face the green eyes glowed
and cast a magic spell about.
Such art before has never flowed
from sculptor, I began to doubt;
but there the nymph-like form remained
a perfect shape, a lovely thing!
"How can mere jade," I then complained,
"have any power to rule anything?"
Still, I was spellbound by the stare
of the jaded statue standing there.

I strained to see each measured stroke
and each new marvel thus provoked,
for it appeared this work contained
a touch of genius that is rare.

I saw the sculptor press again
his grinding tool, working with care:
down both the arms and slender hips
grinding and polishing as the strips
and sparks, they flew along the floor,
and thus the work grew more and more!

Now that the time was drawing near,
you heard the Master's voice declare,
"It's time to show my handwork fair
that all men's eyes may marvel there!"
And now all day and night was heard
the grinding and the polishing sound,
as in the shop, the sculptor stirred
while time now o'er him surely hung.
Day by day he faltered not,
nor sleep nor drink could make him stop.

Then one night I watched intensely
because the work had reached its end,
and I was eager to see a happy
face I was sure I would commend;
but, no, the face I saw looked ghastly!
And, O, the voice I heard was grave:
"I've failed. I've failed! A curse on me
and all the years of toil I gave!
In spite of all my practiced skill,
I lack the gifted power still."

The green-eyed statue carved in jade,
the lifeless lady that he made,
just stood there in the lamplight's glow
with shining, cold, rigid green brow!
The sculptor held a hammer in
his hand, madness o'erpowered him,
and shattered o'er the dusty floor

the jaded statue forevermore—
then wept while all the pieces there
lay glittering in the lamplight's glare!

Then something happened that seemed strange.
The anger on his face was changed.
His weeping eyes, they wept no more
and turned their gaze from off the floor
as if his troubled mind was soothed
by some silent, mysterious truth.
I heard him say, his raging ceased,
"I am...I am...the masterpiece!"
And with bowed head he walked away,
and was not heard of since that day.

## If I Could Save Up Time

They say that time is money.
Well, if I could save up time
like some people save up money,
I would bank a lot of mine!

Think of all the time I've wasted,
that I've surely thrown away.
Imagine if invested
what it would be worth today!

I wouldn't even want the interest;
all I'd want are those lost years
that I whiled away and wasted
on an empty bag of cheers!

Yes, they tell me time is money;
but if I could save up time,
I would give to someone worthy,
who ran short, a bit of mine!

And I'd live some moments over
with the wisdom of today,
when the wine is so much sweeter
and a little goes a long, long way!

**Young Wayne Malik**
(Dedicated to Wayne Malik Cooper,
who died at the early age of nineteen)

Toll on, you bells, let wide your message spread!
Your dirges, let them ring! Sad, sad the sounds
that sweep the air and in the hearts abound:
"Break! break!" they peal, "Young Wayne Malik is dead!"
Dead ere his prime and so much left unsaid!
So many dreams unborn and songs unsung;
so many deeds that shall remain undone,
and promises that are forever fled!

Yet—should we grieve who see not past the veil
nor understand God's glorious plan ordained
for all who sleep and who await His call?
Man's purpose is so empty and so frail!
We serve God's will, and no death is in vain,
for we, to live, must die; to rise, must fall.

**I Sing For Clara**
(Dedicated to Clara Watley-Paige, who departed
on Saturday, May 27, 1989 after a brief illness)

O sisters of the sacred well
that lies beneath Jove's throne,
begin and let your hymnals swell
and give this poem tone!
I come to bid farewell to one
who now is summoned home!

I sing for Clara Watley-Paige!
We must not let her essence dear
be swept away without fair wage
of some melodious tear!
I sing for Clara, who would not?
O may her deeds not be forgot!

She loved people, both old and young,
and was a tireless doer
for those whose causes are unsung:
the young, the weak, the sick, the poor!
She loved and in return was loved
by all who knew her here and above.

She knew to sing and was an avid reader!
With pen and wit, a gift for words,
she was a natural leader
who aimed only to serve
her fellow beings before going on—
O what a champion!

Compassion, charity, and love,
deep faith in God and family,
these are the things she was made of
that perish not eternally!
Come, sing for Clara, who would not,
that her good deeds are not forgot!

And though the bitter tears may swell,
though heavy burdens may still cling,

a greater wisdom now compels
this kindred heart and mind to sing:
"A life that was a light shall be
a light unto eternity!"

**Steady the Drumbeats Roll**
(Dedicated to young Mark Gaskin...R.I.P.)

Heavy the bells they toll
sending their echoes far-flung!
Steady the drumbeats roll,
steady they roll and long!
Sadly the sounds unfold,
was he too old or too young?

Was he a man or a child?
Bitter the fate that befell
him who walked here a short while
and paid so dearly to tell
what it must cost being a child
and being a man as well!

Somehow the two must part
and yet remain as one;
but to the innocent of heart,
it is so hard to belong,
harder to follow the chart
and to be weak yet be strong!

Ever painful the grate,
too many choices to choose;
often bitter truth comes too late
after the weak are abused—
to cope thus with cruel fate
always to win is to lose!

He was a child at heart
who groped to be a man,
playing the dual part
that not too many can.
God knows the road is hard,
what with a losing hand!

Was he born late or too soon?
Could it have been otherwise?
Some can dance well to the tune;
others may not be so wise

and pay the piper too soon!
Out of step, how can they rise?

Was he born late or too soon?
When was the world any different?
It has no time and no room
to be so kind and so patient
with those who are not in tune,
with those who are weak and innocent.

Somewhere between child and man
many are hopelessly cast,
groping the best way they can,
fighting a battle they've lost!
He was a child in this land,
now he has paid the highest cost!

Heavy the bells now toll,
sending their echoes far-flung!
Steady the drumbeats roll,
steady they roll and long!
Sadly the sounds unfold
for one who died too young!

**Earth Angel**
(Dedicated to Maria Wood)

Sweet were the smiles that dwelt upon her face
as radiance dwells on flowers poets praise!
Worthy the heart, worthy the loving ways
that made her life endearing to our race!
Ever her kindness, thoughtfulness, and grace
flourished even during her bleakest days!
She was the best in all of us, one phrase:
*Earth Angel* fits her life lived on this place.

Now we shall find her absence hard to bear,
shall grope to fill the void and ease the pain!
"Why do the good die young?" the mind inquires;
but be consoled, long life's no blessing here,
or else a rose would live and die in vain!
To serve Him well is all that God requires.

## O Gentle Warrior
(Dedicated to Fred Wason)

It seems just yesterday we chatted awhile!
Now gone forever the flame that once shone bright,
the calm, gentle demeanor, the cheerful smile
that formed the essence of his spirit and light.
O gentle warrior, your battered will was tested
until the end, as ours, too, shall be
before the flame of life from us is lifted—
it is the price of our mortality.
O fellow traveler who is laid to rest,
whose earthly shell once housed so many gifts,
sleep; sleep in peace, for you have given the best
within your power to give, and shall be missed
as long as memories live and the past is told
by those who knew and loved you since days of old.

## Roland
(Dedicated to Roland Watson, friend and former classmate)

He is gone! Our noble friend is gone!
Look not for him, O look no more,
until the past becomes the future
and Death's mystery at last is known,
until a bridge across the abyss
shall make the past and future one.

He is gone! Our noble friend is gone!
All that he ever was is gone!
The brilliant mind, the intellect,
the subtle wit, the quiet tone.
A thinker, shy, not much a talker—
his true feelings were seldom known.

Life of the party was not his fame;
crowds and fanfare were not his game.
Yet I would choose him for my captain
to head my best debating team;
and I would trust him though he remained
at times unyielding to extreme.

His brave, courageous, embattled soul
sought, on his terms, his terms alone,
to face life and to face death whole!
Not whimpering, not even one plea,
unwavering, bidding death take hold,
he passed into eternity!

Now he is gone! Our noble friend is gone!
Look not for him, O look no more,
until the past becomes the future
and death's mystery at last is known,
until a bridge crosses the abyss
and makes the past and future one.

**Thank You, Professor Bob**
(Dedicated to Dr. Robert E. Beecher)

A quiet giant who could walk
with kings and still remain humble,
a man of intellect, thoughtful
and kind, a wise and gentle man
such as you seldom find, he was
a brother to his fellow man,
role model, teacher, advisor,
always sensitive to the needs
and thoughts of others. From his lips
harsh words were never spoken.
He had a way of listening calmly,
of speaking in a mellowed tone
that made you feel at ease and know
he was your friend whom you could trust.
He was a master of the art
of gentle persuasion. Never injuring,
never offending, he could win
you over with a smile and drawl.
"Well now, you may be right," he'd say,
or, "Yes, I see your point, but on
the other hand..." and very politely
he'd make you see some subtle fact
you never even thought of,
or somehow might have overlooked.
He was sought often by his peers
to speak at social gatherings,
and he became one of the wisest
and best loved of our elders.

His young associates and students
called him Bob, which he liked,
rather than professor or doctor.
Added to all that has been said,
I cannot speak highly enough
of him who was a friend and mentor.
I knew him since I was twelve;
he was my teacher in grade school,
In junior high, in high school
and in post-secondary as well.
He saw my transformation from

163

a once truant, grade school brat
to a most improved student and scholar,
imparting knowledge, debating issues,
becoming a teacher just like him,
and one of his colleagues and friends.

But I have yet to thank him for
a treasured gift he gave to me
and do so now belatedly.
One day back in the summer of
nineteen hundred eighty-seven,
I received a small brown envelope
addressed to me and stamped three times
as if the sender was making sure
it reached its destination!
Opening the envelope, I found
a note and some old photographs,
pictures taken long, long ago,
as many as four decades or so,
when a classmate invited a group of us
and our teacher, Bob, to spend our vacation
at the home of her parents,
the Reverend and Mrs. Ephraim Alphonse,
in Bocas Del Toro, Panama.
While there, the group of thirteen went
from Bocas Town by sea to an island
in the Caribbean called Cusapin,
an Indian village in a remote,
unspoiled place. Though adventurous,
we took to the wilderness and to
the native village and the sea
with cautious curiosity.

This was the closest to nature
that most of us had ever been,
and we marveled at that unspoiled place
so far from all the comforts and
conveniences that we had known;
but it made such an impression that
upon returning to Bocas Town,
for days we talked about the trip,
the Indian words that we had learned—
kukemuko (companion), muko (friend)

164

mo toboto ari (you are wise)
and kobo kobo (good morning)—
also the things we ate and saw,
the scary nights and scary sounds,
the wind in the trees and the night creatures
shrieking, perhaps trying to scare us off
high in the hills of Cusapin!
It was a most thrilling adventure,
and it was also fun to see
how easily Professor Bob
had mingled and made lasting friends
with the natives of Cusapin.

For many, many years since then,
nothing could top that island stay.
Tempus fugit, as always,
for that was fifty-plus years ago
when I was only nineteen!

I held the envelope, looked at the date,
believe it or not, and couldn't believe it was already
twenty-one years that had gone by
since he sent me that envelope
with a note and twenty-eight photographs
in black and white that he had taken
as an amateur photographer
in June of nineteen forty-seven.
He kept them forty years ensconced
in his own box of memorabilia!

I looked at the envelope again
and realized the startling fact
that it was just before his death
when he had sent those photographs
knowing how much I would treasure them.
It was the kind of thing he would do,
and it was the last time I heard from him.
He must have known the end was near,
and I like to think it was his way of saying,
"Here's a gift for you, young 'fella',
something to remember me by!"
I noticed the handwriting seemed quite weak
near the end, as if he strained to finish

the note, as if he had run out of time.

I looked at the photographs again
that for all these years I had forgotten
existed, and, being deeply moved,
I traveled back into space and time
and relived that summer of long ago.
Thank you, Professor Bob!

## Flower Unsurpassed

(Dedicated to my beloved sister, Fermina (Fifi) Edghill
who departed April, 1999)

To have known her gentle smile,
her trusting, honest ways,
her genuineness of person,
her sweet and generous nature,
her thoughtfulness, her kindness
in words as well as deeds,
who could know her and not love her?

With a soft and gentle radiance
bringing so much warmth and joy,
she possessed the special blessing
of a true and loving heart;
she gave of her inner beauty
like a flower unsurpassed,
and exchanged it for a crown!

"Flower frail, flower fair,
flower that God planted here
to bring joy into this world,
now your earthly days are over,
all your wages paid above,
God has called you home, dear sister,
to eternal peace and love."

**Le Adieu**
(Dedicated to Maurice Heywood)

We know that some day we, too, shall depart
as sure as morning follows after night,
or autumn must give way to winter's right!
Yet when sorrow o'erwhelms the human heart
because from us a dear friend has to part
and no more shall their presence greet our sight,
we who have no power over dark and light
and cannot comprehend the unseen chart,
nor yet the Hand that moves us through the unknown,
what our minds can't breach, we must let be,
for only faith can transcend understanding.
O friend, the One who made you calls you home!
Your course is done! Your spirit is now free
to join the Heaven's choir echoing!

**O Captain! O Captain!**
(Dedicated to Laura La Bon Higgins, former
Director of the Manhattan Educational Opportunity Center
who returned home in November, 2003)

O Captain! O Captain!
How pale and still you lie!
No more your valiant spirit
shall guide our ship at sea!
No more your voice shall sound
its clarion call so clear!
No more to set the bar for us,
to cheer us on to newer heights
and goals year after year.
No more to inspire and upbraid us,
to console us and to share our personal grief.

O Captain! O Captain!
How pale and still you lie!
Too swift, proclaims the heart,
too swift the dark night came
and stole you from our helm!
You've led us well over rough seas
and fought so many battles
with mighty pen, with matchless wit,
with courage and with wisdom—
and never lost a fight—till now!

O Captain! O Captain!
How pale and still you lie!
We've seen you wrestle this last foe
and watched you bend but still not break,
and prayed for our dear captain
that you might win this battle yet
and be yourself once more—
but that was not to be!

O Captain! O Captain!
How pale and still you lie!
How many orphaned dreams and thoughts
and visions that once flourished,
are now forever fled
from so brilliant a head!

We might have shared those dreams,
alas, who shall pursue them now!
O Captain! O Captain!
How pale and still you lie!
No more your love for children shall you manifest,
no more to hug and cuddle them in your arms!
We watched you give your heart to them
time after time and never tire as they returned your love!
And to your friends and staff your kindness knew no
bounds,
nor your compassion for others facing hardship!
You were so strong—and yet so gentle.
You were so firm—and yet so fair.
You were so great—and yet so humble.
You were so serious—yet light-hearted.
You were the exemplar of a friend,
a fighter, leader, lady, all in one.

O Captain! O Captain!
How pale and still you lie!
When shall there be another
like you to guide our ship!
You knew this ocean like a book:
this city, this town, the people in it, great and small!
You knew the who, where, when, what and how
to pave the way and get things done!
And how you loved this Harlem and the people in it!
And how you loved this school, this ship The EOC!

O Captain! O Captain!
How pale and still you lie!
Thanks to the keel you helped to build,
this ship shall still sail on--
but what of you, my Captain, what of you!
I pray, throughout the years to come,
may we never forget you!
O well that we should honor you,
your life was like a light
that shall shine throughout eternity!

**Just as You Are**
(Ines' favorite hymn was "Just as I Am" by Charlotte
Elliott, 1835)

So generously she gave her heart, her being,
her worldly possessions, everything she had!
In fact, if you could classify people
into two groups, the givers and the takers,
you can be sure she'd top the givers list.
As far back as can be remembered,
she always had a weakness (or a blessing)
for giving and for forgiving, for believing
and trusting people to a fault, often
trusting so much that she was easily
taken advantage of, and never would
she even notice! No matter how often
this would occur, her nature stayed the same.
She'd never see or even try to see
the faults in others, as if hoping perhaps
that if she kept on giving and kept trusting,
in the end people would change their ways—
their conscience would somehow cause them to change!
I know some might consider that as foolish,
at best naïve; the fact is, Ines was
the kindest, most unselfish human being
I ever knew—too kind, perhaps too gentle
and far too good in nature for this world!
Goodness like hers too often is abused
by others and too often is exploited.

She never did complain about anything,
about the meanness, cruelty around her,
and least of all, how others treated her.
She never even winced or spoke about
her own suffering and pain. Often she'd be
feeling excruciating pain, yet if
you asked her how she felt she'd always say,
"I'm feeling all right," though you knew she wasn't.
She kept her suffering to herself as if
to her, her whole life was a kind of penance—
or sacrifice to endure until the end.
Like Job, she'd bear it all, however harsh,
and she would wait patiently for God's judgment,

171

knowing that when He called He would find her
true to that heavenly nature that He gave her.
This world could take away all her possessions,
all her material goods, all that she owned,
even her flesh and blood and still not take
away her goodness of heart, kindness of soul,
trust in above. The first things they can take;
the latter she shall keep with her in Heaven.
O my dear sister, genuine and true!
O patient, giving child of God, return now
to your Maker! He will give you peace
and your rewards which you richly deserve,
"just as you are, without one single plea!"

**Death Has No Sting**

The fallen leaves lie scattered on the ground;
the gentle rain this sad occasion greets;
the damp grass bears the tread of solemn feet;
hardly a sight, hardly a worldly sound
that does not lend its harmony profound!
This is the hour, the place where friends now meet
who come to bid their last farewells with sweet
memories of one who sleeps; here, gathered 'round,
the sad assemblage joins in hymns and prayers
and hears the scripture read by one who leads
and lends comfort to those who grieve the most.
But should we weep and dwell upon our tears?
Joy comes tomorrow, so the scripture reads;
death has no sting for us after the cross!

## Questions

Why are there things our eyes can never see?
Why do we dream and wish for things to be?
Why are illusions? How far is the horizon?
Why do we need opinions to rely on?
How high's the sky? How vast are all the oceans?
How many stars are there up in the heavens?
Why do things change and, as we know, need to end?
Why does time pass and never come again?
Why came we here, to where shall we depart?
What of the soul, the mind, the living heart
when life has ceased? I asked and ask again,
why are there things we cannot comprehend?
Why do we grope for answers since our birth
and in a moment we are gone from earth?

## We Shall See

When summer's gone and, with it, youthful plays;
when solitude beclouds late autumn days;
when once-fair daisies have all passed their prime,
and glories are lost in forgotten time;
when dawns are turned to dusk, blue skies to gray,
and tired warriors dread a chilly day;
when dry leaves wither and ripe fruits decay,
and mighty arms and backs have lost their sway;
when speech falters and soon heartbeats must stop
for Death who cannot wait to claim our lot,
despair not that this shell will soon be gone!
It was not meant for us to keep too long.
One curtain closes and another opens wide,
then we shall see what's on the other side.

## The Old Man

His drooping eyes, which once were gay,
speak of a world that's dead and gone,
when youthful hearts were lent to play
on some long since abandoned lawn!
Sad, pale old man, how fleeting time
has robbed you of your Spartan prime!

His faltering voice speaking with pains,
once, tremulous, could rave and shout
like Triton blasts in vibrant strains
when he and comrades romped about;
but now how spent, how very faint
that same voice speaks in soft restraint!

His shaking hands that, limp, hang down,
helped build the future of this land,
with sturdy strength once tilled this ground
and in their fullest crowned a man!
But tempests drained their stalwart strength,
caused them to bend and shake at length!

His puny frame heaped in a chair,
cuddled 'neath shawls to keep him warm,
in whose eyes, weary, comes a tear,
knows now, at last, the bitter storm
as he awaits there patiently
the last sleep till eternity!

How frail you are, O flippant life,
the ravages of time to bear!
Eventually both pain and strife
shall rend you in their ruthless snare,
and cynic death, smiling aside,
shall make of you his charming bride!

## O Tired Heart!
(Dedicated to my father, Cornelius R. Evans)

O tired heart that longs for rest,
that longs for, yet that dreads to sleep,
your plight moves not earth pitiless!
Ah, better that you taste a deep
quietus, end all nights and days
and shun this mortal coil that weighs!

O tired heart, your visage dims;
you've lost the fire of better days
when you had championed lofty dreams
and played a part in lively plays!
One part remains, one exit nears
to mark the close of all the years!

O tired heart! O battered will!
Your citadel in ruin lies!
Your troops have vanished o'er the hill!
Your banner fades against the skies!
For you the drumbeats soon shall cease
and crown you with eternal peace.

O tired heart that longs to rest,
how did it all become this way?
How did you come here so far west?
Your dawn turned into dusk of day,
your leaves, once green, now crisp and brown
and fallen withered on the ground?

O tired heart caught in the stream
of some eternal time machine
that writes our lives across a screen
where features change scene after scene,
your moments were not meant to last,
no sooner born and they are past!

177

O tired heart that longs to sleep
but dreads to leave loved ones behind
and treasures which you thought to keep,
nothing remains but shall decline—
even the oak must bend its head
and one day nestle in its bed!

So, tired heart, dread not to sleep,
for sleep shall end all mortal pain
and carry you across the Deep
where heartaches shall not rise again,
where there shall be no mystery
nor mention of mortality!

### O God, Estoy Muriendo

(Dedicated to my brother, Hubert M. Evans, otherwise known as "Lamb." I wrote what I believe were his last thoughts as he was dying. The last words he uttered in this life were, "O God, estoy muriendo!")

"I see fields of clover,
pastures green
on the other side
of a quiet stream!
Will I taste the clover?
O God, estoy muriendo!

I'm so tired and lonely,
don't know what to do!
Can't find my way, if only
I could hold onto you,
then I wouldn't be so lonely!
O God, estoy muriendo!

Remember when,
long, long ago,
you held my hand and then
said, "I love you, bro,
big bro, my best friend"?
O God, estoy muriendo!

I never forgot!
I was your right arm!
So many times I fought
to keep you from harm,
no, I never forgot!
O God, estoy muriendo!

Remember how
I could make you laugh?
How you cackled with joy
till your belly band burst!
Who'll tell you jokes now?
O God, estoy muriendo!

179

Last time we met here,
we were brothers three,
traveling everywhere;
happy and proud were we,
frowning on despair!
O God, estoy muriendo!

You came from far away
bringing me gifts;
but the best gift, I say,
was seeing you! What a lift
it gave me that day!
O God, estoy muriendo!

We were three brothers who
were united again!
I held onto you
lest I fall from the strain!
Now the brothers are two!
O God, estoy muriendo!

No one understood me
better than you!
You promised to see me
again; I waited, too!
But Fate said, unkindly,
"Hoy estas muriendo!"

Look at the clover!
And those pastures green!
So easy to reach over
And bathe in their scene!
Why struggle? Why bother?
O God, estoy muriendo!

I can smell the clover!
It's like long ago
when life was so tender
and songs were so mellow!
Where's my little brother?
O God, estoy muriendo!

The light is fading away!
When you come again,
my bed will be clay!
Will my leaving offend?
Will you miss me, I pray?
O God, estoy muriendo!

I see fields of clover,
pastures green!
Now I'm crossing over
that silent stream!
I love you, my brothers!
O God...estoy muriendo!"

## Child of the World

Child of the world, where have you been?
Where in the wilderness have you been?
How did you come to be lost from the fold
way out there in a foreign land,
way out there wretched and empty and cold,
poorer in spirit than a soul that is damned?

Child of the world, lost, gone astray,
pitiful sibling of man gone astray
deep in the dens of iniquity,
where abound shadows no one can hold,
where there is naught save insanity
and greedy Mammon trying to capture your soul!

What were you seeking, what was your goal?
What was your purpose till now never told?
What did you hope in those dungeons to find?
Did you not know, could you not surmise
while you were risking your soul and your mind,
that you were the victim, you were the prize?

Child of the world, where have you been?
"I've been to the gates of Hell and within,
seen all the trimmings, the trappings and more,
listened to the demons who tried hard to lure,
then nearly losing myself evermore,
suddenly I ran with my soul out the door!

I ran, yes, I ran with my soul out the door,
everything else left behind on the floor—
my lust, my greed for the things of this world,
my vanity and pride as I fled that hell hole!
I looked back in anger, still haggard, and hurled:
"Not my soul, no, never, not my immortal soul!!"

182

## Truth Seekers

It is hard to remember what we were like
before we became what we've become,
before we set out to find truth, and found
that we lost it even before we'd begun,
that truth existed in a place where we
were happy without even knowing why,
when we saw perfection as we see no more
and we knew not the things that we now know,
when we were yearning to become,
when we were young and innocent!

It's hard to remember what we were like
before we became what we've become!
We were curious and so eager to learn—
truth seekers without a clear purpose or plan—
and what have we learned after seeking so long?
Very little except that to where we began
in the end is where we must return,
and the poet was right who once said,
"The child is father of the man,"
for the truth we have missed is, as years pass by,
perfection was ours before we were wise
when purity of vision was given to us,
then taken away swiftly as if by plan!

## The Man, the River, the Bridge and the Moon

One day for a final assignment in his class
a teacher gave this challenge to a student,
"Here are four subjects: moon, man, river, bridge.
Using iambic pentameter verses,
you are to go home tonight and write a story
based on these four subjects I've given you.
Feel free to use your own imagination,
but the story must not be less than four pages
typewritten or one hundred forty verses,
or one thousand two hundred sixty words!
This paper will determine your final grade!"
Overwhelming as this was, nevertheless,
the next day the student handed in the paper
to the teacher who had expected him to fail
since he was not a good student in class
and always seemed distracted and somewhat lost!
Surprised by such promptness in completing the task,
the teacher took the paper and started to read:

"One moonlit night the figure of a man
stood on a bridge, the center of the bridge,
his hands grasping the rail, his eyes transfixed
upon the choppy waters far below!
What brought him to this place, this time of night,
this cold and lonely place when he could be
somewhere else warm and cozy? What circumstance,
coincidental or purposed, brought him,
the bridge, the river, and the silvery moon
together in that fixed moment in time?
It could not be a lovers' tryst, indeed,
for such a place seemed treacherous, too exposed,
and he was not there with a lover's mien
or happy expectation, judging from
the sadness in his eyes, and his fixation!
What, then, could be the reason? Let us be
the wind, or night, and listen to his thoughts:

"For years I've sought and chased in vain
phantoms, symbols, fool's paradise and things
for which men vie, strive, suffer, even die;
I've struggled blindly till I found myself

184

in a place I did not know, a state of being
too alien to be mine! I could not see,
I could not recognize myself! Who is
this person, I inquired, that looks like me,
that walks like me, and even talks like me,
this person whom I swear I do not know,
who grasps at shadows, beats his brains against
imagined walls, who gropes, who struggles, climbs,
who falls, who hastens to his own demise,
not knowing it alone is his reward
and not some phantom prize! Who is this being,
this self-deluding being who tells himself
that things are ends, defined in terms of his
primordial appetites, and, furthermore,
possessing them he lives, and is fulfilled,
when all he has is emptiness? Who is
this creature flailing, raving, fussing with
himself, causing a big to-do, as if
the universe takes note, or cares what suit
he wears, what car he owns, what house is his,
or what he had for breakfast? Who then is
this creature, this mere fleeting speck, who builds
a citadel around himself and says, 'I am
the master, ruler of all that I survey,'
who worships monuments to self and sounds
his own brass bugle, bellows, rattles loud
a little while, a second and then crumbles
and turns to dust that's scattered in the wind
like all his monuments, or else becomes
substance to enrich the earth beneath him?
Who is this hapless creature anyhow?

And so I found myself down this dark road
where I once thought I knew the way, not seeing,
just fantasizing; but the darkness leads
only to darkness, and dreams are tricky when
the dreams come from the root of man's dilemma,
and are but opiates to romanticize
the tragedy and let us think that we
grasp some great illusory prize. Who is this man
who on this road of darkness having slaved,
who having fought, scratched, suffered, worked so hard
and still no prize? He dares impugn what he

185

calls 'fate,' that catchword blamed for everything,
that easy answer, tired excuse, when all
it does is alienate himself from self,
increase the pain and hasten his demise.

Now, face to face I stand with this dilemma:
I see no way—no way!—I can't go on,
not on this road, this dark, this empty road
that leads nowhere! O God, is this what life
is all about? Is this all that there is?
Here, then, I make my stand! This tired brain
and body cry, No more—better the cold
and friendly wave than to continue thus!'

And as he set himself to plunge, feet first,
into the murky waters, a gust of wind
blew in his face, the lapping waters cried
out from below, 'No, no, no, do not jump!
Spare me the agony of watching you
sink low beneath my depths, gasping for breath,
grasping, clutching the life you throw away
too hastily! No, no, wait, do not jump!
I've seen too many before you; but you,
at least, I implore before you jump, for yours
is not a lover's cause, or pauper's cause,
or one who's burdened with a crime, you seek
for meaning of your life! Wait, do not jump,
you will not find it here!' He hesitated
for just a moment, looking blankly at
the cold and murky river, doubting his senses.

He looked around, but there was no one there,
only the night and silence! It was then
the bridge cried out, its shifting girders straining
in the tossing wind, 'Ho! Stop! Listen to me,
I've stood here many, many years, built by
a dreamer! Many have crossed o'er me, countless
the throngs of goods and people! I have felt
good serving thus, but I was never built
to be used by you this way! Wait, stranger, wait
before you jump! Think earnestly about
the life you throw away! If he who made me
made something good, think of yourself, and who

made you! You will not find the answer here,
nor in the river far below, so I
implore you, do not jump!' The moon peaked out
from behind a cloud, watching sadly to know
her light shone down on such a scene. Often
she has looked at men below destroying themselves,
serving the masters lust, greed, vanity,
and pompous power. No wonder so many
are lost, like this one, aimed at self destruction.

The stranger looked up to the moon and said,
'It's all so good and well for you, you shine
your light on all below and you have purpose
and meaning!' But the moon answered and said,
'And what about you? What about you? You curse
the darkness where you walk, but you have chosen
darkness! Can't you see, you, too, have light,
a different kind, perhaps, only you don't
even know it! I cannot shine my light
into men's hearts, into their minds, into
the darkest caverns of their souls! My light
is nothing compared to yours! The light of God,
that is your light, the brightest light of all!'

Those words touched something deep inside! He held
his head, trying hard to quell the turmoil there.
He searched now deep within where the truth had been
buried so long, and then he realized
the river below was right, and the bridge was right,
and the moon shining above in her wisdom
was right, for he never looked towards the light
while he was groveling all these years in darkness!

Then...turning his head that was bent low in shame...
he looked up suddenly to the sky and said,
'Very well, from now on I shall seek the light!'
And at that instant o'er the darkness rose
a sweet auroral light that Heaven exposed,
that seemed like nothing he had seen before!
So moved, he walked away into the dawn,
into a brand new day, a new beginning!
And the river was glad, and the sturdy bridge was glad,
and the moon, beaming, was very, very happy!"

The teacher finished reading, profoundly moved
and lost for words! He paused for just a moment,
looked at the student mystified and said,
"Thank you!" It was all he could manage to say;
then took his briefcase and quietly walked away!

## Before They Are Gone Away

Where will we go
when there's no place to go
without a reason or rhyme?
How will we say
words we failed to say
before they were lost in time?

What will we do
when nothing we can do
will solace the heart and mind
when the best and dearest,
the first and the fairest
have left us here behind?

No earthly treasures,
no earthly kingdoms,
palaces and pleasures
we could offer as ransom
can bring back our loved ones
long after they are gone.

When there was time
and reasons and rhyme
and so many words we could say,
we had neglected
what we regretted
and now time has flown away.

Only a longing
that is remaining,
a longing so tender
for the vessel once filled with wine!
We cannot refill it, only remember it
here in the heart and mind.

So don't let loved ones,
parents, daughters and sons,
siblings, wives, husbands, and friends
dally while you delay.
Tell them today
you have something to say,

don't wait till they have gone away!

Tell them now
while time disposes,
tell them here and now.
It's the easiest thing to say.
Tell them now,
let them smell the roses
Before they are gone away.

## In Such a Place of Timelessness

When you are quiet enough to hear,
sometimes it is the strangest thing
that comes into your head,
if you are listening

and all the world is nowhere there.
It may be just your heart beating
or the stillness while lying in bed
of eternity calling.

In such a place of timelessness
within the land of nod,
between deep sleep and consciousness,
my soul speaks soft to God.

Although His voice I may not hear,
yet as my soul is speaking,
deep in the silence everywhere
I know that He is listening.

# Winter Poems

## To Winter

O winter, can I help it if
you have a tainted reputation
in certain circles, speaking of
the tropics where I come from!

What's with your polar bear and musk ox?
To me walruses have no appeal,
and you can keep your arctic fox,
your moose, your reindeer and your seal!

I do not take to caribou
and could never live like an Eskimo
who sleeps inside an ice igloo
and eats blubber and loves the snow!

Mind you, there's nothing wrong with that,
and I suppose that an Eskimo
would hate my warmer habitat
with its scorching, humid scenario!

Believe me, when the mercury dips
below seventy, I wear a coat,
and my hands freeze without warm mitts;
but if I'm dressed in a bearskin coat,

winter is not bad to have around,
with the Christmas trees and the bright décor
and a cup of hot chocolate going down!
In fact, I think I'd like it more!

## A Winter Miracle

O lady, my sweet lady love,
you came into my heart one day
just like a newborn butterfly
that from its chrysalis emerged,
and brought with you ebullient light
and warmth to fill a wintry night!

O lady, O sweet lady love,
you came into my heart one day,
and then I thought I was transported
for just a while to paradise
to taste and be tempted by bliss,
to dare to dream of what could be,
if only for a little while,
when on your lips I placed a kiss
and felt the murmur that your heart
in that brief time returned to me!

O lady, O my lady love,
you came into my heart one day
and gave me hope and hints of joy
that my glad heart strove to contain!
Was it unreal, was it a dream
that happened that December night?
Was it a fantasy that played
a tender tune, a silent song,
then flared up like a glorious flame
that once a lifetime comes along?

O sweet lady, O my lady love,
you came into my heart one day,
"A winter miracle," I said,
and doubted it was really true
at first when, reeling, my heart swooned
to know that it could bear such joy!
Alas, it was a dream, a dream I say,
though it had seemed so real to me!
She came into my life one day,
a lady young and beautiful,
a phantom, took my breath away,

and then, alas, she went away!

Why did I think that at this stage
I had a right to know such bliss,
that such a miracle could be
to cause a pure and honest joining
between a butterfly of spring
and one trying to turn back the page?
And yet, for but a little while,
I lived just such a fantasy
when two hearts one December night
embraced each other passionately!
The stars shifted, the earth it moved,
the goddess of love ignited, then,
fearing that she had gone too far,
parted two hearts that felt her fire!
She sent my lady love away
and cold again is December!

## When I Was Young

When I was young and passing seventeen,
I was quite shy and also very green.
I met a girl whose name was "Dancing Doreen";
since she taught me, a dancer I have been.

When I was young and tried to be a dandy,
I met a girl I called, "O my, Miss Mandy."
She was so fine she was like sugar candy,
and I was thrilled to be her Handy Dandy.

When I was young, and I was slightly handsome,
I courted quite a few fine, lovely lassies!
I met a girl whose name was "Cherry Blossom,"
and she was so much sweeter than molasses.

When I was young, and I was somewhat carefree,
I met a girl whose name was Caroline!
I showed her things; the things she showed to me
I cannot tell, but they were so divine.

When I was young, and I was not too choosy,
I met a girl whose name was "Dizzy Suzie,"
she took me for a ride, it was a doozy!
She left me breathless and a little woozy.

When I was young, while passing through Delancey,
I found the place was not too very fancy.
I met a girl there by the name of Nancy,
Who made me change my mind about Delancey.

When I was young while dancing through the tulips,
I stopped awhile to admire their regalia;
I took one home, but soon her nagging lips
made me sick of tulipomania.

When I was young, and I was very strong,
I met a girl I called "Hard Time Yvonne."
I never slaved so hard or tried so long
to win a prize before from anyone.

When I was young I thought I found true bliss,
I met a girl I called "pro forma" Lorna.
She was a beauty I could not resist;
later we parted, O but that "pro forma."

But I have no regrets at all today;
I loved them all, and they were good to me!
Though we have parted, this much I will say,
we drank the honey—and now must let it be!

## Farewell to Youth

Farewell O youth, O prime of life,
you had your day, but not for long,
one season only, that was all,
and now just memories for a song.

You took from life all it could give,
but time cannot sustain desire—
nor can youth's ghost raise pastures green,
and relight a once brilliant fire.

The best that life can offer now
is real enough to warm the soul
and calm the seas of changing tides,
but lights no more the fires of old.

Where once dwelt rich, green summer fields,
is now late autumn's bleak domain.
Where vibrant sinews once prevailed
only their remnants now remain.

If we could change our destiny
and alter our mortality,
know that I'd never let you go,
O youth, it's time that set you free!

## Some Things We Should Not Pray For

I heard my father say
before he went away,
"Be careful how you pray
and what it is you pray for!
It might surprise you one day
in a mysterious way!"

I wished I had been wiser
and listened to my father,
but I was only ten
and prayed that I was thirty.
But when I got to thirty
I still didn't comprehend.

I prayed and prayed again
and wished that I was fifty,
but when I got to fifty
I wasn't happy then.
So I prayed that I was sixty,
and do you know, at sixty
I wished that I was ten?

## The Old Men's Club

There is an old men's club
made up of travelers passing through
who meet sometimes along the way,
be it at sunrise, noon, or dusk of day,
and stay awhile revisiting
old themes and tales of yesteryear.
They are travelers, each on separate paths
yet moving in the same direction,
who started from a common place
and journeyed far since they began,
travelers who have so much to tell
about events since they last met,
about the past and friends they knew—
some who are gone and some remaining
but growing fewer and fewer still.
They are travelers older and wiser,
slower from traveling and from wear,
who see in each their own reflections
of triumphs, trials, and despair
that take their toll inevitably;
and from their meetings each one gains
some insights till they meet again,
or their journeys come to an end.

Tell me, who really are these old men?
Aren't they the same boys turned old men,
who once could run and never tire,
could race the wind and shout like thunder
and soar like eagles on the wing
without a hint of growing old?
Aren't they the same impetuous youth
who once thought they could wrestle fate
and vanquish fears with phantom powers,
who once thought they were their own masters,
presumptuous youth of untried valor,
who boasted like there was no pain
existing that they couldn't endure,
no mountain that they could not climb,
no challenge that they could not conquer!

O youth, O flippant youth untested,
you are nature's trick to fool all men,
to make them dumb before they are wise,
and when they are wise wish they were young!
O devious Time that lets us frolic
knowing full well that sooner or later
we shall extinguish like a flame,
no sooner lit than gone forever.

O welcome, shadows of vanished youth!
O welcome, valiant old men, welcome
to that distinguished club ordained
that all must join who travel here.
Welcome, until your journeys end.
Welcome, welcome, old men.

## Spring, Summer, Autumn, Winter

Here's to the memories of spring
when life was mellow and songs were new
and we first wakened to its calling—
it was the best time that we knew.

In fact, it was the closest ever
that we had come to Eden's shore,
when we would run and never tire
and dared winter to reach our door.

Youth's brilliant garden was a-blooming
and happy days had taken root;
the vines were strong, the trees were grooming
and branches readied to bear fruit.

Then came spring's sequel, summertime,
when Nature's children were full grown;
when seedlings, at last in their prime,
tested their powers until well honed.

Summer brought mating, parenting time
when Nature's work was at its height.
Seedlings birthed seedlings in their time,
and day was longer than the night.

Gardens were flourishing in the sunlight.
Whoever thought of autumn then?
The earth was good, the future bright,
moving along—time seemed a friend.

But summertime gave way to autumn,
as spring gave way to summer, too.
And autumn soon must give the baton
to winter who awaits his cue.

Blow, blow now, frantic autumn winds
and scatter leaves once green, now brown.
O fateful autumn that reminds
us spring and summer days are gone.

Maybe you're not to blame but, O,
you bring sad thoughts, as your winds blow,
of friends and loved ones who are no more,
who once shared joys of long ago!

You hint of cold blasts and winter snow,
O autumn, while your changing hues
show us how hard it is to let go
the joys of youth that we must lose.

Wait, wait, O winter, I insist!
Let not your bitter cold chill come.
Compared to you, autumn is bliss,
and does not freeze a lily pond.

O but a few friends still remain
to face the winter of old age.
How many shall we see again
after life's bitter winter's rage?

## Who Will Be the Last to Cry?

If all the flowers die, who will cry?
Who will cry for a summer rose
or a daisy when its life is closed?
If there are no more flowers and leaves,
who will cry for all of these?
And if all the people we once knew
and loved, including me and you,
should die, who will cry?

I cannot bear to think of it
or glean the consequence of it.
If all the flowers that we knew,
all of the girls and boys, too,
who filled the gardens of our youth
should all be gone, the bitter thought
that makes me sigh
is—who will be the last to cry?

## Swan Song

Within the realm of nature,
all species know when it is time
to return again to their maker.
Some may protest or try to flee,
although it will avail them not;
some go without a sigh or whimper
as death o'ertakes their weary lot.
But one greets death magnificently.
I speak about the muted swan
that through its life sings not a note,
yet when the end is close at hand
sends from its bursting lungs so sweet
a parting song or plea to God,
not in protest but exultation,
as if to say, "Here I am, Lord,
your prodigal child returning home,"
and, folding its wings, closes its eyes,
then slumps, lifeless, to earth and dies.

## A Winter Sonnet

Autumn sends out its sweeping breath, announcing,
"Now put away your summer things and pleasures."
Creatures are busy storing away treasures
for needy days knowing that winter's coming.
And when the dreadful cold on earth is pouncing,
they know, while sleeping, winter's drastic measures
though dreadful pass, and soon glorious new pleasures
will rise and will be greeting them in spring.

So why are we afraid of winter's coming
and pine that summer days for us are gone?
It is as natural as the swallows leaving,
and there may yet be a glorious new beginning
after the blistering winter's course is done.
It must follow, if winter, then comes spring!

**John Weldon Evans** was born in La Boca, Canal Zone and graduated from La Boca Normal Training School in 1948. He taught in the Canal Zone "colored schools" until 1956 when he migrated to the United States and there furthered his education and career. In the United States he achieved a Bachelor of Arts and two Master of Arts degrees. He worked as a lecturer in mathematics and subsequently as Associate Director in charge of Academic Affairs and as Interim Executive Director at the State University of New York Manhattan Educational Opportunity Center, administered by the Borough of Manhattan Community College. After forty years of service, he retired in 2009 from SUNY-MEOC and has since been devoting his full time to writing which was put on hold for a number of years. **Spring Turns Too Soon to Winter** is his second book. His first book, written in 2008, is entitled **Songs and Stories of a Digger's Son,** Published by TJMF Publishing.